2020: My Last Hope

Book 3 of 5

Douglas Schnapp

We Are the Company We Keep

Ensign reached Lansing in the afternoon. The sky was gray. Mindset matched the dreary weather. Clouds shrouded the city, a metaphorical manifestation of Ensign's mental state. Ensign felt a storm approaching.

People were walking all around outside the shopping center. Tammy was standing on the pavement, at the curb by the traffic lane. She was looking for Ensign. Ensign muted the stereo as he pulled up. He pushed the button to unlock the door. Tammy slid into his car.

Tammy and Ensign matched gazes. Ensign sensed the turmoil in Tammy's thoughts. He knew things had gone off the rails. Ensign saw confirmation in Tammy's eyes. If he had been there in Lansing, could the drama have been avoided? Ensign thought about his avoidance of the scene in Lansing, Michigan. He knew avoidance had been the right choice. He was relieved he hadn't been around for the drama.

Tammy didn't have the luxury to leave the city whenever she felt like it. Ensign felt a twinge of sympathy for her as he saw the desperation in her eyes. Her demeanor added to the gray and overcast day. Ensign tried to remain positive. Something caught his attention.

Tammy's right hand was wrapped up in bandages. Ensign asked why. Tammy told him. As she began to tell a story, Tammy unwrapped the bandages from her hand. Ensign looked over to a horrific sight; Tammy's hand was shredded and mangled. Tammy's entire hand was a display of human anatomy. Ensign saw the layers of meat down to the bones. He saw tendons, ligaments, and all the intricate details of the insides of a human hand; details that should never be exposed. Ensign was aghast. With his eyes open wide, Ensign asked Tammy if she needed medical attention.

"I'll take you to the hospital right now..."

"No. I'm not going to the hospital."

Tammy rewrapped her hand with the bandages. Ensign's eyes remained open wide. His mouth, dropped open as well. Ensign decided not to push the issue. He wasn't sure why Tammy refused medical treatment, but he decided it wasn't his business.

Ensign had only been gone a brief time, but the atmosphere in Lansing was volatile. Ensign purposely avoided and ignored any drama when he was in the city, but the drama seemed to have a way of finding him and pulling him back in. It was Ensign's bad luck that day; Tammy had fallen out with Dan a week prior. It was his luck that the two of them were still at odds. It was Ensign's fate to pick up Tammy; in hopes she could lead him to Dan.

The first place Tammy wanted Ensign to take her turned out to be a shady apartment complex; only a half mile from Dan's recently vacated house. Ensign remained in his car as Tammy ran inside to pick up whatever it was that she needed to pick up. Ensign would later read about an incident at those apartments, taking place months later; in December of 2020. Those apartments: where Tammy used a butcher's knife to stab a guy in the heart, killing him on his balcony ...allegedly.

Tammy and Ensign pulled from the parking lot to the surface streets. Ensign prepared the hotrail tray while Tammy was inside the apartment. Ensign blew down a large line of crystal and passed the tray to Tammy. Tammy stopped about halfway through her line. She looked at Ensign; exclaiming how the line was too large to finish in one pass. Smoke poured from her mouth as she shook her head. Ensign told her to finish her line. He wanted to do more, and he needed to dump more crystal out on the tray.

Tammy and Ensign spent the rest of the afternoon driving up and down the streets of Lansing, Michigan. Ensign drove, and he prepared the drugs...Tammy did her thing on her phone to attempt to locate Dan. As the light in the sky began to fade, Tammy received confirmation of Dan's location. She gave Ensign an address. Ensign typed the address into his GPS. Ensign was ten minutes from Dan's location.

"I'm going to make a quick stop."

Ensign went inside the rest stop to use the bathroom and the vending machine. He came back out to his car. Ensign cracked his windows as the two of them filled the car with meth smoke. Ensign broke up another eightball on the tray...and his hand twitched, dumping the crystal all over the floor of his car. Deciding it to be a lost cause, Ensign dropped another eightball of crystal on the tray. The two of them each blew down a hotrail line. Ensign then pulled from the rest stop; back on track to find Dan. He was six minutes away, according to his GPS. It was late evening, and it was dark outside.

Tammy's mangled hand resulted from an incident at Dan's house earlier in the week. According to Tammy, that incident caused the rift between her, and Dan. Ensign pulled into the complex of town houses. To avoid potential violence, Tammy advised Ensign to leave her on the opposite side of the complex. Ensign stopped his car and let her out. Tammy assured Ensign someone was on the way to pick her up. Ensign thanked her for the help, and he drove alone to the other side of the neighborhood of townhouses.

Ensign found the specific address, and he parked his car in the driveway. He grabbed his backpack, and he tapped underneath his shirt; being sure his handgun was accessible. Ensign anticipated others being in the house with Dan. He didn't know who or what else to expect.

Ensign knocked on the front door, and he waited in the dark

for someone to open it. The porch light flipped on. The door swung open. Ensign's eyes met Wolf's eyes as Wolf answered the door. Ensign had never met Wolf before, but he knew exactly who he was when he saw him standing in the doorway. The stories Ensign had heard over the prior months convinced him that he never wished to meet Wolf in person. "So much for that," Ensign thought to himself.

"Wolf...is Dan here?"

Wolf already knew who Ensign was, as well. Wolf greeted Ensign and shook his hand.

"Ensign, come in. He's in the basement. Have a seat. Help yourself to food or drinks from the refrigerator if you wish. You're welcome to whatever you can find."

"I'm good. Thank you."

Wolf pulled out a chair in his kitchen for Ensign to sit down. Ensign took a seat. Wolf went down to the basement to find Dan. Ensign sat there in the kitchen and wondered who else was in the house. A girl, someone Ensign had never seen before, walked into the kitchen from the left side. She glanced at Ensign as she hurried her way out of the kitchen, through the door on the other side of the room. Ensign heard footsteps as people walked up from the basement. Wolf appeared first through the doorway. Dan was right behind him. Ensign stood up.

Though Ensign had only been away from Lansing for a brief time, it felt as if he hadn't seen Dan in years. It was as if Dan had aged a lifetime in the few short weeks Ensign was gone. After their initial reunion, both men took seats at the kitchen table. Wolf left the kitchen to go back to sleep in his bedroom.

"So...I've heard some things. I figured it'd be best if I came back and found you. I'm not concerned with the BMW. I wanted to be sure you were all right..."

Ensign watched Dan. Dan began to explain what all happened

in Lansing in Ensign's absence. Ensign could tell Dan was stressed; a new stress Ensign hadn't seen before. He could see Dan was paranoid. There was an air of desperation in Dan's voice. There was worry. There was a seriousness which showed him Dan was gravely concerned with his immediate future.

There had been violence in the city...with more expected. There had been a series of events which resulted in the death of an individual associated with an overlapping social circle. There had also been bulletins on the local news; reports that law enforcement sought Dan and a mutual friend for questioning in relation to a crime caught on surveillance video. Two completely separate situations; both weighed heavily on Dan that evening in Wolf's kitchen.

Dan and Ensign sat at that kitchen table for multiple hours as Dan filled Ensign in on the drama unfolding in the city. Ensign was again thankful that he practiced distance and anonymity in all things related to Lansing, Michigan. His concern was for Dan's wellbeing. Ensign felt like Dan hadn't told him all the details of all his situations, but Ensign didn't push the issues. Ensign listened to all he was being told, and he assured Dan he would help in any way he could.

"I can't believe you came all the way back from the South to find me and make sure I was alright."

"I love you, man. You know that."

"I love you too, man."

As Dan told Ensign he loved him, Dan began to cry. Ensign felt bad for him, but he felt there was still something Dan was holding back. Dan and Ensign hugged again, and Ensign walked out the front door. Whatever else going on with Dan was meant to come out at another time...or not at all. Ensign got in his car and left Wolf's house.

He was back in Lansing, Michigan, and dread crept into his mind. He knew his time in Lansing had a quickly approaching expiration date. He knew it was time he began to plan an exit strategy. Ensign's time in that city was overstayed. He needed to tie up any loose ends…while he still had the chance.

By Proxy

Dan maintained a low profile once Ensign returned to the city. Ensign saw him from time to time. Ensign assumed Dan was with Ashley and Brittany during the times he didn't see him at the usual locations. Ashley was on the video from the local news; she was in the surveillance clip alongside Dan. Brittany, Ashley's best friend, had sent Ensign the news clip while Ensign was down South.

Luke

Luke was twenty-five years old. He had been looking for direction in his life. Luke was separated from his long-term girlfriend and son. He was hoping to better himself, and he anticipated rebuilding a family dynamic with them. Though Luke and Ensign were consuming crystal together multiple times a day, though the two of them were in the streets together running business, though their associations frequently involved shady people and criminals, Ensign felt something positive in that new friendship.

Luke just spent nine months in rehab for a heroin addiction. Ensign commiserated, knowing heroin addiction all too well himself. Luke was off the heroin, but he remained close to the needle. Hanging out with Luke gave Ensign an excuse to return to frequently shooting drugs.

Over the next weeks, Ensign became close friends with Luke. Luke was out of rehab and back in the streets of Lansing. Though Ensign hadn't seen Luke since that night he first met Dan a year prior, Luke and Ensign became inseparable after their reunion in spring of 2020. Ensign helped Luke work on his car. Luke helped Ensign work on his. Ensign tattooed Luke and some of his friends. Ensign supplied Luke and his friends with fuel to party. Luke introduced Ensign to a whole new circle of people in the Lansing underworld. Ensign put Luke on, and he helped Luke to level up.

"It's a go. He just texted me back."

"Bet. Let me get my stuff together, and I'll be ready to roll after I finish tattooing."

"All right. I'll let him know we will leave here in about an hour."

"This should be fun. I haven't been to the Upper Peninsula since I was like twenty-five."

There were eight people sitting in Caleb and Simon's living room. Ensign was at the dining room table. He had been tattooing his left arm for an hour. Occasionally, Ensign took short breaks to do hotrails. Luke had been texting his friend; one who lived in the Upper Peninsula of Michigan.

Ensign let Luke know he finally had a clear schedule that evening. Luke previously informed his friend of the quality product Ensign had at his disposal. Luke's friend had been pestering him the prior week to take a trip to see him. Until that evening, Ensign was too busy to make the trip. After Ensign crunched some numbers, he relayed a dollar amount to Luke; one which was acceptable as a surcharge for the time, distance, and gasoline it would take to reach the Upper Peninsula and make it back to Lansing. Luke set up the transaction for that night.

Though his Lexus was running, and Ensign had been driving fine around the lower regions of Michigan, he was still waiting for Dan to change out the exhaust system and catalytic converters. Ensign bought the replacement parts, and he had them in his possession. The parts had been there since the previous stretch of time when he was in Lansing. Ensign had been waiting on Dan to be around and available to do the work. Dan owed Ensign a couple thousand dollars. The work on Ensign's car was agreed upon to cut into that debt. Between hiding from the police, and whatever else Dan had been getting into, Ensign couldn't wrangle Dan to do the repairs on his car.

After the hydroplaning incident the previous month, three of the tires on Ensign's Lexus had blown. The thought of driving his car to an unfamiliar and distant location wasn't sitting well. Though the three tires had been replaced, Ensign wasn't sure the fourth tire would maintain integrity on a trip to the Upper Peninsula.

Ensign rented an SUV for the evening trip. He needed to pick the car up from the rental agency at the Lansing airport. A friend dropped him off. With a handgun strapped around his ankle, and drugs in the backpack slung over his shoulder, Ensign walked into the airport to sign paperwork and pick up the vehicle. He wasn't crossing through the terminal to any gates, so he didn't need to pass through any security checkpoints. Ensign was handed the keys for the rental SUV. He left the airport and stopped back at Caleb and Simon's apartment to pick up Luke.

Peristalsis

"If life gives you aids…make lemon aids."

Sometimes, even the best solution to fix a predicament won't give you a resolution which makes everything as good as before the predicament began. Life becomes different. What reality was; then becomes just a memory. What reality then is; something different, having been altered by the predicament.

"You can pick your battles; you can pick your nose…but you can't pick your battles' nose."

Sometimes, it doesn't make sense to try to solve an issue. Life throws things at people which show them it's time to step back, evaluate, and move away from a current course. When you think through your next moves, and no move will give you a net-positive outcome; it becomes time to cut your losses. It becomes time to move on…

Ensign had been overhearing talk of a list; actually, two lists. He hadn't paid much attention when he caught random whispers in passing. The day came when he overheard multiple people, at various times and at various locations, mention those lists. Ensign was sitting in a bedroom with Luke and five other people when he heard Luke tell one of his friends that the lists just came out. Ensign asked Luke a question.

"What are you talking about a list, or lists? I've heard them mentioned before."

"I'll send them to you. Every so often, higher-ups put out two lists. One is a snitch list, and one is a hit list."

Ensign didn't press the issue. A moment later, he received a notification on his phone. Luke sent Ensign both of the newly released lists. Ensign read the names on each of the lists. Ensign remembered Dan, in his recent spiraling paranoia, had mentioned to him that he was worried he was on the hit list. Ensign didn't see Dan's name anywhere.

Ensign didn't recognize anyone's name on the snitch list. He was close with one person on the hit list. It was Ashley; the friend on the news story; the surveillance video with Dan. Luke and his friend group had a rivalry with Ashley and Brittany. Something happened between them, positioning them as enemies. Ensign stayed out of it, so he didn't know the specifics. He didn't want to know the specifics.

Ensign sat on one of the couches in Jerry's living room as he noticed the clock. It was three in the afternoon. Ashley and two of her friends were in Jerry's kitchen making sandwiches. Dan and Jerry were near Ensign, sitting in chairs in the living room. Two others were on another couch. Ensign sat, and he listened to the people having random conversations around him. He was deeper in thought than he cared to express at the moment. It was three o'clock in the afternoon.

Ensign wasn't paying specific attention to any one conversation. All the words from everyone in Jerry's house washed over him, as he caught bits and pieces of different conversations. Dan stood up from his seat and headed to the kitchen. He stopped for a second in front of Ensign. Dan turned to him.

"Are you alright, man? You're extra quiet..."

"I'm good. I'm just thinking."

Dan looked at Ensign for another two seconds as he

considered Ensign's response. Dan then nodded his head. He continued on his way to the kitchen. By three o'clock that afternoon, Ensign had heard enough to put him in a weird headspace. Every person in the house that day was engaged in standard interactions with each other. The bits of conversations Ensign heard had all added up to a vibe which made him feel some kind of way.

Ensign heard people discussing their plans for the upcoming week, plans for the near future, and plans for the summer; conversations he had heard many times before. The words, that day, held more weight than they had previously. There was something about the casual way everyone was discussing upcoming life...

Ensign thought on it for another moment. It wasn't so much about everyone discussing upcoming life; it was the fact that life would go on unabated, and Ensign wouldn't be there for any of it. It was three in the afternoon. Without saying a word to anyone, Ensign stood up and walked outside to his car. He wasn't yet completely checked out of Lansing, Michigan, but he was remarkably close...and he knew it.

The Wisdom Within Victor's Monster

Lee and Ensign sat in Ensign's car in a parking lot in Howell, Michigan. Ensign's friend Lee worked a third shift job. The time came for Lee to leave and head to work. Lee managed to compose himself over the previous hour, since he injected that large shot of crystal. Had he not talked Lee into doing just half of the amount he originally wanted to do, Ensign figured Lee wouldn't have recovered at all.

Earlier in the evening, Lee tried to convince Ensign that he had been doing shots of full grams of crystal. Ensign flat out told Lee that he was either measuring wrong, injecting an extremely inferior product, or that Lee was lying to him. Ensign asked Lee to explain his process. He shook his head as soon as Lee told him how he measured the doses. Ensign was genuinely annoyed when Lee explained his process. He heard the same claim from others before.

"I crush up the crystal and fill the syringe all the way to the top line on the barrel. I use a syringe which holds a full cc, so each mark is a tenth of a..."

"Stop talking. How can you even think that's anywhere close to accurate? Those lines measure liquid. What if you crush the crystal more one time than another? What if you compress the powder more one time than another? What about the density of crystal? What does volume have to do with weight?"

Lee stared at Ensign. He had no answers. He sat and thought to himself for another moment. Ensign knew what Lee was about to say. Ensign kept his mouth shut and waited for the inevitable next words to spill from Lee's mouth.

"I'll do a gram of your stuff right now..."

"Again, stop talking. You absolutely won't do a gram of my stuff in a single shot. I'll properly weigh you out four tenths of a gram and prepare it correctly. I'll weigh it on a scale. I'll draw it up through cotton from a spoon. Four tenths will be enough to get you high beyond what you claim was a full gram shot."

It took Lee right up until he had to leave for work before he was able to articulate the errors of his previous technique. Ensign made sure Lee knew the seriousness of being accurate when measuring drugs. Lee stepped from Ensign's car and walked across the parking lot to his parked car. Ensign started his car, and he pulled from the parking lot.

There was a rest stop on I-96, just outside of Howell, Michigan. After Lee and Ensign parted ways, Ensign decided to stop off for some chill time and an ice cream sandwich. Ensign was in the habit of frequenting rest stops while he traveled, and he knew that particular rest stop had the good ice cream sandwiches in the vending machine; strawberry ice cream in between two cookies. Ensign made it a point to stop at the rest stops he knew had the good ice cream sandwiches.

After an hour of sitting in his car; doing hotrails and interacting online, Ensign decided it was time to leave the rest stop. He thought about it for a second and chose to step from his car to walk back into the service center for one more ice cream sandwich. Ensign picked up his wallet from the center console, and he gathered up some loose trash from his front seats. He walked to the vending machine and bought the item of his desire. He then walked his bag of trash over to one of the garbage cans. Ensign threw out his garbage and headed back across the parking lot to his car.

Ensign left the rest stop. He planned to head to Ohio and sort through items in his storage unit for the remainder of the night. Ensign planned to leave the storage complex in the morning. He was then going to spend the next three days in Fort Wayne, Indiana with a lady he had been interacting with online. She had a dominant personality, and they had discussed a fantasy which they planned to realize together.

The sky was beginning to lighten the next morning as the Sun was rising. Ensign was sweaty and exhausted. For hours, he had been sorting, organizing, searching, and digging through all the items in his storage unit. Though the drugs kept him awake, Ensign was physically drained. He decided to gather up the items for travel and take off for Indiana.

Ensign pulled the storage unit's overhead door closed and organized his things in his car. He was hungry. He hadn't eaten anything since the ice cream sandwiches at the rest stop that prior night. Ensign decided to order food and pick it up on his way out of Perrysburg. He reached toward the center console of his car to grab his wallet. It wasn't there.

A flash of panic washed over him as the memory of throwing away the bag of trash at the rest stop entered Ensign's mind. His wallet had been in his hand as he tossed the garbage in the can at the rest stop. He remembered it clearly. What he didn't remember was seeing his wallet at any point after he threw away the trash.

Ensign combed his pockets. Nothing. He searched everywhere in the front of his car. Nothing. His heart began to beat quicker. Ensign postponed his plans to head directly to Indiana from Perrysburg. Over the next two hours, he removed every previously packed item from his car. He opened up his storage unit again, and he sorted through everything he had already sorted the night before.

Ensign looked up information for the service center. He found a phone number online. It was mid-morning at that point, and a rest stop attendant answered the phone when he called. Ensign explained to the attendant that he was fairly sure he had either thrown away his wallet at the rest stop, or he may have dropped it in the parking lot. The rest stop employee had Ensign hold as he went to check to see if anyone turned in the wallet to their office. Ensign waited with fingers crossed.

The attendant came back to the phone. He told Ensign he found nothing. Ensign's sense of panic grew inside him. He let the attendant know he was going to return to the rest stop within the next two hours. The attendant told Ensign he would keep a lookout. Ensign hung up the phone. He forgot about being hungry.

Ensign spent what was left of that morning, and early afternoon, at the rest stop. He looked everywhere he had been the prior night: the parking lot, the lobby, the bathroom. Ensign waited until the night shift employees came to work at three o'clock that afternoon. They told Ensign they hadn't found anything on their shift the previous night.

It was a week later, and Ensign again planned to head to Fort Wayne, Indiana to stay with the lady he met online. A few hours after he left Lansing that Friday afternoon, Ensign crossed over the border from Michigan to Indiana. He received a phone call from a number he didn't recognize as he approached his destination in Fort Wayne. Sometimes, Ensign answered calls from unknown numbers...other times he didn't. Ensign answered that phone call as he drove.

"This is Ensign."

"Hi Ensign. This is Officer Johnson of the Michigan State Police in Brighton, Michigan. We have…"

"No way," Ensign interrupted the officer. "You guys found my wallet? Please tell me you found my wallet."

"We did," the officer answered.

"I can't believe it!"

Ensign was thrilled. He hadn't cared that he had three hundred and fifty dollars in cash in the wallet, and he had already cancelled his bank cards. Ensign's recovered drivers' license was what made him the happiest. It was two months into the coronavirus pandemic. Government offices and services were basically inaccessible. It was doubtful to downright hopeless to think he would have been able to get a replacement drivers' license without extreme complications and delays…if at all.

"I had three bank cards, my New York apartment identification badge, my license, and three hundred and fifty dollars in cash in the wallet…"

"It's all still there."

"Dude…I'm in shock. Thank you so much. I'm out of town right now, but I'll be there after the weekend to pick it up. Thank you, for real. How'd you find it?"

"It was anonymously dropped off by a guy earlier today. He brought it in and left."

"Amazing. I'm shocked there are still other honest people out there. I'll see you on Monday. Much appreciated. Again…thank you."

"You're welcome. I'm happy we could help you out. See you Monday."

The officer on the phone sounded as happy as Ensign had been when he delivered the news to Ensign. Ensign was beside himself. He pulled into the apartments where the lady in Fort Wayne lived. Ensign smiled to himself. After he parked, he took a minute to post on social media about the situation. Ensign wrote that with all the bad in the news going on at the time, there were still good things going on…even if not significant compared to everything else.

Ensign thought about the whole situation. He had been seriously planning his exit from the scene up in Lansing. His drivers' license was crucial to making his exit. Ensign spent that whole week not knowing how he was going to manage not having his license. He knew he had to leave Lansing. He knew how important it was to spend no more time than necessary in that toxic scene.

Ensign breathed easier knowing he would soon have his license again. Had the police not called him, Ensign would have had only bad thoughts of being stuck longer in Lansing. Ensign sighed with a breath of relief. He grabbed his backpack as he stepped from his car, and he switched his focus to meeting that dominant woman; the lady with whom he was about to spend his weekend.

The drive back from Fort Wayne, Indiana was full of reflection. Ensign thought of what had become of his life: his travel over the past couple of years, his consumption of crystal, his time in Lansing, and his sexual exploits. The dynamic that weekend, with a woman deep into the BDSM scene, had been enjoyable. Though he had been about that life, Ensign's body felt the results of the woman's desire to do things to him as she pleased. That feeling served to remind Ensign he had belonged to her over the previous couple of days.

Ensign blew down one more hotrail as he exited the highway in Brighton, Michigan. He pulled into the police headquarters and parked his car. After about ten minutes inside the building, Ensign walked back out to his car; reunited with his wallet and its contents. Again, Ensign was amazed his wallet had even been recovered. He was more amazed that his license, bank card, and all the cash were still there in his wallet.

Since his bank cards had all been cancelled, Ensign was then stuck waiting on his new cards to arrive by mail to his friend Jane's house in Ohio. Ensign expected a phone call from Jane in the upcoming two weeks to let him know his new cards had shown up. Lansing was still Ensign's home base until he had his new bank cards.

Ensign decided, right then, that he would leave Lansing for good as soon as he received those new bank cards. No exceptions. Ensign felt happy with that decision. His days were numbered. Ensign wasn't sure the exact day he would be gone, but at least he had an estimated time frame...a very short time frame.

Fast Years of Long, Slow Days

Ensign reached Jerry's house in the late afternoon. Simon and Caleb's apartment had been Ensign's jump-off point in East Lansing after Dan no longer had his house. Jerry's house was Ensign's spot on the opposite side of the city. Though Dan was only around sporadically by May of 2020, Ensign was most likely to run into Dan at Jerry's house.

Jerry

Ensign first met Jerry at Dan's house the previous year. Jerry was a gay guy in his mid-twenties. Ensign didn't know how Dan knew Jerry. One morning in 2019, Ensign woke up in Dan's living room, and Jerry was there. Jerry ended up getting into a lengthy conversation with Ensign about how he needed to process and manage his feelings from his fiancé dying in a recent car accident.

Though he had no interest in anything sexual with Jerry, Ensign could tell Jerry was into him. Ensign made it clear that the feeling was completely one-sided. Jerry conceded the issue, but he also asked Ensign for a favor. Ensign listened to his proposal, and he told Jerry he was willing to help him out.

"Dan had told me you are well-versed in the weird and the taboo. I've always had a fantasy of being peed on."

"I can do that for you. I'll make it happen. I'm going to video it."

Ensign told Jerry he'd be ready in thirty minutes. Ensign told Jerry he'd let him know when it was time. Jerry went into Dan's bedroom. Ensign went to the kitchen and filled up an empty two-liter soda bottle with water from the sink. He drank half of it right away. Ensign managed to drink the other half ten minutes later. Another ten minutes later, and Ensign felt ready to go. He did all he could to hold off for yet another ten minutes. Finally, Ensign could take it no longer. Ensign knocked on Dan's bedroom door.

"Jerry let's go. I don't care if you keep your clothes on or not, but you need to get to the bathtub quickly. I can't wait any longer."

Ensign set his phone on the windowsill in Dan's bathroom. Jerry stripped naked and got on his knees in the bathtub...

Afterward, Jerry thanked Ensign for the experience. Ensign zipped up and walked out of the bathroom without saying a word. Later, Ensign sent Jerry a copy of the video. Jerry replied with one word.

"Hot."

Ensign continued to see Jerry periodically at Dan's house. Jerry and Dan made money streaming live videos on a social media platform. They had a makeshift studio in Dan's basement which they utilized to make content. When Dan lost his house, they moved the studio to Jerry's basement. Dan also moved into Jerry's house.

When Ensign arrived at Jerry's house on the evening he recovered his wallet, there was already a group of people there; friends and others he knew. They were all preparing food and setting up to have a cookout and bonfire that night. Ensign settled in. Other people continued to arrive for the cookout at Jerry's house.

Though Ashley had her own business going on, due to the quality of Ensign's product, she was always a customer of his for personal use. Ensign sat with Dan, Ashley, and Brittany in an upstairs bedroom; hotrail after hotrail consumed off of Ensign's silver serving tray. While certain other people trickled in and out of the bedroom that evening, anyone Ensign didn't know remained outside at the bonfire. Ensign had no desire to interact with people he didn't know, and his friends were well aware.

Waiting Out the Clock

While on the trip with Luke to the Upper Peninsula of Michigan, Luke told Ensign a story. Luke was convinced he had been given a "hot shot" by a higher-up the day before he entered rehab nine months prior. The "hot shot" was a syringe of heroin designed to cause Luke to overdose. Luke was sure someone had wanted him out of the way. Ensign asked Luke who had been with him that day. Luke told Ensign his best friend Brad had been there. Luke also told him Brad had known that Luke was going to be given the "hot shot."

Ensign spent an afternoon with Luke in a parking lot in Lansing, replacing a valve on the fuel line of Luke's car. They finished the repairs as the sky was almost dark and the mosquitoes were out in full effect. Both of them were sweaty and dirty from the work they had done. Luke told Ensign to follow him in his car. They had a stop to make before they reached their next destination that night.

After they picked up what they needed to pick up, Luke and Ensign each drove their own cars to their destination for the night. As Ensign parked his car on the street behind Luke, Luke got out of his car and jumped into Ensign's passenger seat. Luke had also heard the gunshots as they were parking their cars on the street. Two more shots rang out, and the two of them slumped lower in their seats.

Silence filled the air for a moment. Luke and Ensign decided to stay in the car and stay low. Moments later, Luke and Ensign heard police sirens approaching from behind them. Ensign sat up after the lights and sirens passed by his car. Ensign saw two police cars blaze around a corner two streets up from where he was parked; the area where the shots had been heard. The sirens cut off, but the red and blue flashing lights continued to reflect off of the houses two blocks in front of them. Luke and Ensign both stepped from Ensign's car and walked up to the side door of

Brad's house.

The story Luke had told Ensign about the "hot shot" echoed in his brain as they walked up to Brad's door. Though Luke was convinced there was nothing to worry about, Ensign still wasn't fully comfortable knowing that Brad had known about the attempt on Luke; the person who was supposed to be his best friend. The story was just one of many examples of the scene in Lansing, Michigan; examples which Ensign had either heard from others or witnessed himself. He knew he was close to being out of that scene forever. He didn't want anything to come between him and that goal he had set for himself, the goal of permanent distance from Lansing.

Ensign had never seen the process before, but he knew what it meant to "shake a bottle." He had never needed to be involved in any sort of manufacturing. Ensign was also never in need of small quantities of crystal. He had sampled multiple friends' different personal supplies of "shake and bake" on occasions. Sometimes the quality was surprisingly good. The chunky powder even approached the lower end of Ensign's exceptionally high standards for the large crystal rocks he always dealt with. Ensign had also never seen the manufacturing process of those large crystal rocks. He was always on, but Ensign was one step removed from the initial creation.

As he sat and watched Luke's friends "shake a bottle," Ensign did hotrails of his brand. Whether their final product would manage to register on his radar of quality didn't matter. Ensign wasn't going to be there a few hours later to try it out. He had a trip to take that night to pick up more of what was guaranteed to be top tier. As he sat and watched the beginnings of what would get Luke and his friends high in his absence, Ensign began to think about his routine of traveling around the country.

He shook off his daydreams of travel. Ensign's trip that night was business. Those trips were straight to the point. Rarely did he detour at all on those business trips; on those first legs to his destination. Return trips, once he re-upped, often involved many stop-offs to deliver.

It's Not Used, It's Me

As those in the house were lounging around, and while one of Luke's friends was hard at work manufacturing future drugs, Ensign stood up and wished everyone a good night. He let Luke know he would be back the next day. Ensign walked to the door to leave. As he stepped outside to the front yard, he heard footsteps behind him...

Jade

Ensign met Jade a couple of nights prior. Jade knew one of the guys in the house. Luke and Ensign were in awe of Jade's oddly outgoing and bubbly personality when she showed up in the living room, seemingly out of nowhere, in their world. Jade didn't seem to fit in with the rest of the usual crowd. Jade was tall and beautiful. She had an undefinable quality about her. All the people in her presence seemed to vie for her attention. Jade was drawn to Ensign from the beginning; partly because Ensign didn't fawn over her like everyone else. Gushing wasn't ever Ensign's style. Luke pulled Ensign aside that first night to let him know how interestingly hot Jade was to him. Ensign agreed with him completely.

As he began to turn around, Ensign felt Jade's hand on his shoulder. His eyes met hers. He couldn't help but think, in that moment, how pretty her eyes were.

"Where are you going? Can I go with you?"

Ensign thought about both of the questions Jade just asked him. It may have been weakness; he was lost in her beauty as they stood face-to-face. It may have been his weakness at that moment, but Ensign already decided to let the scene unfold to its logical conclusion. He knew full well that he was breaking one of his cardinal rules when it came to his security involving the drug business...but he gave into the moment.

"I have to make a run. I won't be back until tomorrow..."

"I want to go with you."

"Alright...I'm leaving right now. Let's go."

On the way down South, Jade and Ensign stopped off at Ensign's storage unit in Perrysburg. Jade was an impulsive person. She saw an electric hair trimmer in Ensign's storage unit. Jade told Ensign she had thought about shaving the sides of her hair all the way around her head. Fifteen minutes after that, they both got back in Ensign's car; Jade had a new haircut.

Jade and Ensign were gone from Michigan for a full twenty-four hours. They stayed in a hotel, they had sex, they made some videos...and they stayed extremely high. On the return drive, Ensign questioned his lapse in security for bringing someone along with him to a source. Later on, after returning to Lansing, Ensign found out his worries were justified...but in a completely separate way than he anticipated. The issue turned out to be benign.

The ordeal which took place in Lansing in Ensign's absence that night was yet another dodged bullet...another confirmation it was time to leave that city for good. When Jade and Ensign arrived back to Brad's house that next day, Ensign could tell that something had happened in the time he had been away. Luke pulled Ensign aside and told him what went down.

Luke told Ensign a story about associates showing up and trapping out of Brad's house with them until they sold all their drugs...then the associates drugged and robbed Luke, Brad, and their friends. Ensign looked around Brad's living room. The living room no longer had a television...or a stereo. Luke, Brad, and a couple other friends no longer had their wallets, either.

Tick-tock...

Ensign was still in Lansing. He wished to be anywhere else. He needed work done on the exhaust system on his Lexus. He needed to put pressure on Dan to do the work. The hourglass had been flipped over long ago, and the sand was running out. Ensign didn't want to be there when those last grains of sand stopped falling.

Cross Your Eyes and Dot Your T

MSM: Methylsulfonymethane $(CH_3)_2SO_2$...a supplement sold over the counter at drug stores. Luke and Ensign walked the aisles of a pharmacy one morning. Luke had Ensign pick up a bottle of MSM.

"What, is your arthritis acting up?"

"There's another use for MSM. Trust me, you'll see."

After Ensign spent a couple of hours at Brad's house with Luke. Luke dropped a bag into his lap.

"What's this?"

"It looks real, doesn't it?"

"Uh...yeah..."

"It's an ounce. It's yours for buying me that bottle of MSM."

"I don't want that. I have real drugs. I don't want fake drugs."

Luke, Brad, and their friends had a plan. They had been shorted money on a transaction a while back. They used MSM to make fake crystal. They set up a deal with the people who shorted them. They planned to sell the fake crystal to recover their losses. As always, Ensign wanted no part in that. He gathered up his belongings. He had other places to be.

Ensign put the fake ounce in his bag with all of his legit ounces. He didn't know what he was going to do with it, but he was sure he would never sell it. Ensign then forgot about it for a week. It remained in his bag, but in a separate zipper pocket, in front of the real drugs...until one day when it was no longer there.

Luke and his friends had been drugged and robbed. Ensign found out that information when he returned to Brad's house the day after it happened. Ensign too had been robbed in that same span of time. He realized it later on that day. Later that day, when he was at Caleb and Simon's apartment, he noticed one of the compartments of his bag appeared to be empty.

The main compartment of Ensign's bag was still full, filled with the weight he had just picked up; the exact amount he had just picked up. The smaller compartment, the zipper compartment with that single ounce-bag of fake MSM crystal from Luke...it was empty.

During the time with Jade on the trip, she had robbed Ensign. She managed to get an ounce from him; an ounce of crystal...the only fake ounce of crystal ever in his possession. Ensign smiled. Jade had tried. All she had managed to accomplish was to rid Ensign of a useless item; a novelty he was never going to use for anything. Ensign called Luke to warn him to be wary of Jade, should he see her again in the future. She had sticky fingers.

Relational Memory

The next month was tremendously chaotic. Each day surpassed the previous day's level of absurdity. The day finally came; the day Ensign left Lansing, and all the chaos, for good.

Ensign drove south from Michigan. He drove into Ohio. After two more hours on the road, he reached his destination. Ensign hated Lima, Ohio. It was his least favorite city in the state. He made an exception that day. Ensign had been interacting online with an interesting couple. They wished to share intimacy with him. After a week of texting between the three of them, Ensign made another exception: group sex.

Normally, Ensign flat out declined offers from couples. That couple was different. Both husband and wife were very much in love after twenty years of marriage. Ensign understood his role in their dynamic. He was there to enhance the intimacy between the two of them. He wasn't there to "spice up" their sex life, and he wasn't going to be a tool for one of them to invoke jealousy in the other. Both the man and the woman were looking for Ensign to be an enhancement to their already healthy intimate dynamic.

The couple was different in another way as well. Though both of them appeared to be simple husband and wife in their daily lives, their roles switched in the bedroom. The husband, masculine in his daily routine and interactions, became the female in bed. He wore lingerie and makeup, he wore a wig, and he adopted the mannerisms of a submissive female. The wife, as womanly as she was in her day-to-day, donned the role of dominant male in the bedroom. She tied up her hair, she wore the outfit of a blue-collar worker, and she was in charge. Though masculinity and femininity are independent of dominant and submissive roles, the couple lived a standard-role life outside the bedroom; they both fully adopted the traits of the other once the bedroom door shut.

Ensign met the husband at the front door of the house. The husband offered him a glass of iced tea as he led Ensign to the kitchen, where he introduced him to his wife. The couple had asked Ensign what foods he liked to eat in a message the previous day. The two of them invited Ensign to help them finish cooking. Ensign set down his bag, and he helped them finish cooking the tacos they planned to have for dinner that evening.

The three of them talked about life as they ate the tacos. Interests, goals, hopes, dreams...they touched on multiple subjects. Their humor was pleasant. Their demeanor was kind and open. Ensign felt welcome in their home. They discussed their lives, their children in college, their careers. Ensign told them of his former career and of his current travels. He told them how he just left Lansing, Michigan...and how he looked forward to the adventures yet to come.

As they finished eating, their conversation switched to the subject of intimacy. The three of them cleaned up their dishes, and the couple invited Ensign to join them in the bedroom. The wife took Ensign's hand and led him down a hallway. The husband followed behind them. They left the food on the island in the kitchen.

Three hours passed as the three of them shared intimacy in the couple's bedroom. At the wife's urging, Ensign did things which the husband hadn't done before. Ensign helped show them a new level of intimacy. The wife and the husband took turns watching as Ensign interacted with the other. At times, all three of them were engaged together. At one point, three hours into it, Ensign became the one who watched as the spouses made love.

He took that moment as his cue. Ensign told the couple he had worked up an appetite. He then went back to the kitchen to eat more tacos. Ensign sat at their kitchen table and looked out the sliding glass doors into the backyard as he ate more food. Twenty minutes passed while the husband and wife finished with each other in the bedroom. Ensign finished eating as the two of them walked, smiling, into the kitchen to join him for more food.

Ensign had been part of various intimate experiences involving multiple partners. Those experiences mostly fell short of satisfaction. In Ensign's mind, true intimacy always involved one hundred percent focus on a single person sharing the moment with him. Three or more people together always felt distracted, like too much was going on to fully appreciate other people sharing the moment. That time in Lima, Ohio became his one exception; a couple, still very much in love with each other... still very much attracted to each other. A happy couple who invited him to share a small part of their love for each other.

Ensign smiled after he bid them farewell, and he walked out the door. He was happy to share in that experience that day. Ensign checked his phone when he reached his car. Tim had sent him the location of his hotel in Columbus. Ensign set the address in his GPS, and he left his least favorite city in Ohio.

The King of Wishful Thinking

Ensign decided to drive east before he decided to go west. He took I-70 to Columbus, where Tim had been staying in a hotel. As he drove east on the interstate, his phone rang. Ensign answered it. A recorded voice began reciting words.

"You have a collect call from the Shiawassee County..."

Ensign hung up before he heard the remainder of the message from the jail up in Michigan. Dan was trying to reach him. Dan's lies and deceit had burned that bridge. Brittany previously told Ensign of a wild night earlier in the week which landed Dan in jail. Ensign was in no position to bail him out, even if Dan hadn't done what he had done over the prior few months. Since Dan had been lying to Ensign the entire year, Ensign had no desire to accept his phone call.

Before leaving Lansing, Ensign found out Dan had lied to him continuously as he ran up a two-thousand-dollar tab for drugs. Dan went as far as to forge a letter from the IRS which stated his tax refund had a delay. That, after Dan had promised instant payback upon his receipt of the tax refund.

Ensign called Dan out on his lies during an earlier phone call. Dan then admitted he already received, and spent, his tax return. He had strung Ensign along for weeks. Dan took advantage of Ensign's trust in him. Ensign no longer wished to help him.

Ensign stuck his phone back to the velcro on his steering wheel. He texted Tim. Ensign told Tim to send him his room number. Ensign was set to arrive in the Columbus area within the hour. Tim texted Ensign the room number. Ensign turned his attention back to the road for the remainder of the drive.

Tim had been staying at a Sheraton in Columbus for two weeks when Ensign arrived there to see him. After Ensign took a shower, he told Tim to text his plug. Due to coronavirus, the drug market had become unreliable. Though Ensign weathered much of the storm, he had heard talk of entire regions inflating their prices...or running completely dry.

The pandemic affected some of Ensign's sources, so he decided to reach out to his friend Tim. Ensign didn't have a source in Columbus, Ohio...but Tim did. Ensign agreed to the coronavirus mark-up, and they left to go meet Tim's guy in an apartment complex, a location which Ensign had never before been. Tim left the car. Ensign remained in the driver's seat. After a couple of tense minutes, Tim walked back over to Ensign's car and got in.

That meeting with Tim's guy was one of the last steps in Ensign's plan to vacate the Midwest. Tim and Ensign spent the remainder of that night getting high in the hotel room. When he left the next morning, Ensign told Tim he would see him in about a week, when he passed through Columbus again on his way west.

"I'll still be at the Sheraton. Hopefully, I'll be in an upgraded club-level suite by then."

'I look forward to the upgrade. I'll see you then."

Josie sent a text with her address. It was evening when Ensign reached Josie's house. Josie lived off of a major thoroughfare, across the street from a bar. She lived in the Pittsburgh metro area. Josie had a two-story house to herself. It was the first time Ensign met Josie face-to-face. They had been interacting on the website throughout the prior month. Ensign was excited to see her.

Ensign spent three days at Josie's house. At two in the

afternoon, three days after his arrival, Ensign left Josie's house. He continued to head east.

Ensign made it to a rest stop in Somerset, Pennsylvania. He pulled in as the clouds thickened in the sky. Ensign saw the storm coming. He knew it was going to be a bad one. He decided to wait it out. Ensign went inside and used the bathroom before the rain hit. He got back in his car as the first drops of rain began to hit him. Ensign knew he was in it for the duration. He settled in.

The rain and hail began to hit. Ensign pulled out his tray and a bag of drugs. He pulled out his propane torch. Ensign fired it up. He heated the end of his glass stem until it glowed orange. He put the other end of the glass stem to his right nostril. In a sweeping motion, Ensign sniffed through his right nostril, as he plugged his left nostril by pushing his finger against the outside of his nose. Ensign held in the smoke for a few seconds. He then breathed dragon smoke out of his mouth.

As the storm hit, so did the meth. The drug took hold as the large rain drops and hail pelted his car from above. Ensign felt secure in his Lexus cocoon. He felt invincible. As the rain came down, unrelenting outside his car, he was safe in his little world of drug-induced security.

It was June 22nd, 2020. Coronavirus had sunk in, and much of the country's population were secluded in their homes. Ensign had no home. He was in as close to a home as he had. He was in his car. Ensign watched as the parking lot around his car became a lake. The water from the sky was extreme. Ensign opened his car door. He got soaked. He recorded a video for a minute. Ensign then had to close his car door as the water around him continued to rise. He decided it was time to leave before he became stranded at the flooded rest stop. Ensign had to pee again, and he was almost out of gas, but it was time to get back on the road.

Ensign pulled out from the rest stop onto the interstate, figuring it would only be a couple exits until he could get gas and use the restroom. Ensign drove east on the Pennsylvania interstate...and he drove...and he drove. He began to become concerned. Why wasn't there an exit? What was going on? The Sun began to set. Ensign continued driving. His gas gauge was a concern. He watched as the needle began to bury below the red on the empty side. Ensign's anxiety grew...When he googled "longest gaps between exits on an interstate," the following fact came up:

"35.5 miles (57.1 km) between Exits 110 and 146 on I-70 East in Pennsylvania."

His luck...Ensign happened to be on a stretch of road which completely justified the anxiety he felt. He couldn't believe it. His luck on that drive was as bad as it could be. He kept going. His anxiety hit the sunroof. He needed to reach that next exit.

A semi pulled over onto a strip of gravel in front of him, a narrow space on the side of the interstate. Ensign followed behind the truck. Ensign stepped from his car, and he relieved himself on the side of the road. The Sun was setting. The rain was less incapacitating than it had been earlier at the rest stop. With Ensign's anxiety slightly diminished, he zipped up. He got back on the road. Ensign found the next exit as the Sun sank below the horizon. There was no place to refuel when he exited the highway. Ensign white-knuckled the drive back to the previous exit. He got gas.

As he fueled up his car, Ensign reached for his other phone... and he felt an empty pocket. Ensign then felt a sense of panic wash over him. He searched all his pockets; he searched his car...he searched the bags in his car. He remembered seeing his second phone on an end table next to Josie's couch. Ensign had placed it there as he removed his clothes in her living room days before.

Ensign pulled out his other phone. He called Josie. He asked her if she could take a look around for him. Ensign told her one of his phones was, most likely, on one of her tables. Josie immediately told him it was. Ensign told Josie he was on his way back to pick it up.

Though he was originally headed to Philadelphia, the issues while heading east changed Ensign's direction. West...he was meant to go west. Ensign had been to many states out west, but it was time to check off the rest of the states he hadn't yet visited. There weren't too many, but he wanted to visit them all. Ensign also wanted to get out of the drug business. He was far too stressed.

Ensign had made it through the wringer. He had seen those around him fall to terrible fates. He had lost friends to violence, and to incarceration. Time was not on his side. He knew his welcome had run its course. Ensign knew if he didn't sever his ties to the underworld scene, he would soon face an improbability of going on. That world needed to be left behind him. That world needed to become his past. Ensign wanted a life no longer immersed in the drug market. He wanted to be free.

Narcissism

Eight minutes, the light of the Sun must go,
Ninety-six million miles, to reach us below.
I wonder, as I gaze at that orange glow,
Did the Sun burn out seven minutes ago?

Tim's wish had been granted on the day Ensign arrived back in Columbus. While Tim moved his belongings to the new room on the top floor of the hotel, Ensign wired a new amplifier into the trunk of his car, down in the hotel's parking lot. Tim came outside and handed Ensign his new spare keycard. Their keycards not only worked to unlock the hotel room, but they also gave them access to a private club and dining area on the top floor of the hotel.

Ensign was excited to explore the club level and suite in the hotel. The elevator only had buttons for eight of the floors of lodging. As Tim and Ensign stepped into the elevator, the doors closed behind them. Ensign scanned his keycard on the pad inside the elevator. A new floor number lit up on the screen. The elevator took them up to floor nine.

When Tim and Ensign stepped from the elevator, nobody else was on the floor. They stopped at their suite so Ensign could put his bags inside. Ensign took a few minutes to survey the suite. There were two king-sized bedrooms, a living room area, an entertainment area, and two bathrooms in their hotel suite. The entertainment area came complete with a fully stocked bar. It was a shame neither Tim nor Ensign drank alcohol, though the bar itself made a perfect setup to prepare crystal.

Tim's belongings were all in a bedroom on one side of the

suite. Ensign set his bags on the bed in the bedroom on the opposite side of the unit. The two of them left the room to explore the exclusive floor of their hotel. As they walked the hallways, they realized they were the only people staying on the top floor. Tim scanned a keycard on the door to the club-level entertainment area.

The nightclub/entertainment area on that floor of the hotel looked like it was ready to host a banquet or a wedding reception. Ensign recorded some videos in the empty luxury area. Tim and Ensign wandered through the rooms. The two of them hung out in there for a bit. As the Sun began to set that evening, they headed back to their suite to order food from the front desk. The two of them did drugs as they waited for their food to arrive at their door.

As they ate, Ensign received a message from a woman who lived a few blocks from their hotel. She was a pretty African American lady who messaged him after she arrived home from work. She sought a no-strings-attached encounter that evening. Ensign told her he would be over in twenty minutes. The lady told Ensign to walk in; the door would be unlocked...she would be naked. Ensign let Tim know he was stepping out for a short bit.

True to her word, the door to the apartment was unlocked. Ensign walked into the lady's home. True to her word again, she was naked in her bed. She was beautiful. Ensign had no reservations as he saw her, though he did have an issue. He had just injected a hefty dose of crystal right before he left the hotel suite. Though he was thoroughly aroused; as the lady and Ensign began to kiss, he knew he wasn't going to be able to perform.

The lady earlier expressed, in a text message, that she wanted him inside her. Ensign told her he needed to make a compromise. He let her know that he wasn't going to fill her up that particular way. He also informed her of his prowess with his mouth. Ensign told her he guaranteed her satisfaction.

After about a half hour, Ensign's new friend enthusiastically confirmed Ensign had gone beyond what she could have hoped. The lady wrapped herself in a bedsheet as Ensign dressed. She walked him to the front door.

"When's the soonest you can come see me again?"

"Well, I'm about to head out West, probably tomorrow morning. I'm not sure when I'll be back in the Midwest, but I'll get a hold of you next time I'm back."

They kissed again before Ensign walked out into the night. Ensign drove the two blocks back to the hotel with a smile on his exhausted lips.

The Heisenberg Uncertainty Principle

Ensign was back in Lansing. A mix of unusual feelings swirled in his brain as he stepped from his car, into the early morning Lansing air. Ensign had left Tim's club-level suite in the middle of the night. He had driven through the darkness of early morning and reached Lansing as the Sun first began to evaporate the fog from the streets.

The pickup truck was still parked on the road across from the house. It had been sitting there for a few weeks. Ensign previously stopped by the residence and recovered his car's air conditioning charging hose from the front seat of that pickup truck. On that instance, he noted at least three glass stems lying on the front bench seat. There was residue coating the insides of the pipes, residue from smoking methamphetamine.

That pickup truck belonged to a woman Dan knew. Though Dan was in jail, the pickup truck was still parked in the road. The girl who owned the truck still hadn't been able to locate it. Dan had used the truck to commit a crime, and the woman's truck remained there; where it sat since Dan was arrested at the house.

Ensign knocked on the door. He waited. He knocked again. The door opened. Ensign stepped inside. He had been outside that particular house on multiple occasions. He had even hung out there before...just not inside the house. As the front door closed behind Ensign, he noted to Brittany how it was odd that the truck was still sitting there on the street in front of her house. Brittany shrugged as they walked to her living room.

It was still morning as Ensign's last business in Lansing concluded. That particular business normally wouldn't have been worth taking the out-of-the-way drive. Since Ensign always liked Brittany, he made the trip for her that day. Ensign stepped back into his car and pulled from Brittany's driveway around mid-morning.

It was an odd mix of feelings that morning. Ensign felt relief; he was finally at the point of leaving. Ensign felt sadness; despite the drama and stress, he knew he was going to miss many of the people in Lansing, Michigan. Ensign felt nostalgic; he had many important moments and good times during the stretch of time where Lansing was his jump-off point for travel. Ensign felt excited; the unknown and unexplored world beyond the Midwest was in his view.

Ensign's anxiety consumed him as he drove through the surface streets of Lansing. He knew he was literally moments from leaving that chapter of his life behind. He felt it was the perfect time for catastrophe to impede his exit. All the work he did to separate himself from all the negative events which took place around him during that time…Ensign hoped he could manage those last couple of miles in those last couple minutes; incident free…before his life could reset.

He reached the ramp to the interstate. Ensign scanned the road in front of him. Hypervigilant, he checked his mirrors in all directions. Ensign pushed his foot down, and the gas pedal of his Lexus sank into the floor. He blasted off. The crystal ran through his veins, but it was overtaken by adrenaline. The anxiety washed through and out of him on that highway, and it stayed behind him in his past…Ensign's anxiety stayed in Lansing, Michigan.

Though he didn't have a clue what was to become of his life from that day on, Ensign knew it would be like nothing he had experienced. The entire eastern half of the United States was, at that point, essentially his backyard. Ensign knew it up, down, left, and right, North, South, East, and West. He could find his way anywhere based solely on recollection.

He had been to so many places so many times. The roads, the cities, the notable locations…the routes and alternate routes, the markers, the destinations...the best ways through cities and places based on traffic conditions or construction, the most scenic or leisurely paths, or the most time-efficient directions, the ways to avoid tolls, or reach out-of-the-way "secret" locations; Ensign had mastered driving the entire eastern half of the country.

But out West, there were still nine states which Ensign had yet to visit. Ensign decided something right then, as Lansing shrank smaller in his rearview mirror. By the end of that trip, which began at that moment, he would only have Alaska as the single state to cross off of the list. That trip, upon its completion (wherever that then had him land), would end with forty-nine of the fifty United States holding memories of times he spent exploring them.

Ensign did up a hotrail as excitement filled his head. The possibilities were suddenly immeasurable. He felt alive. He felt free. He felt like a person...a person connected to the entire world around him. Ensign felt that feeling he chased his entire life. Ensign felt whole; he was full inside.

In his final conversation with his mom on the night before her death in 2011, Ensign's mom said she was ready to go, but she didn't want to leave them behind. Ensign told his mom to go ahead and go. He told her that she would remain with them, and that he would be ok...

In that moment, as Ensign was driving toward the edge of Michigan in early summer of 2020; in that fleeting moment with the entire world in front of him...Ensign made good on his word to his mom; he was ok.

Phase Potentiation

Ensign took a moment to record video of the incoming clouds. Afterward, he got back into his car and shut the door. In the time it took him to set up a hotrail on his silver tray, the storm hit. Though he couldn't crack his windows to circulate the exceptionally warm air in his car, Ensign decided to try to get comfortable (and fully unclothed) as he waited out the rain and hail.

Ensign was the farthest north in Wisconsin he had ever been. He had been seeing road signs for Wisconsin Dells. Ensign had heard that name before…but he had no idea what it actually was. He looked into it as he did drugs in his car.

At one point, Ensign had an idea. It turned out to be more of a pain than it was worth. Ensign took a towel and some soap, and he walked down a trail behind the rest stop where he was parked. He found a secluded section of dense trees a short walk away from the path. Ensign stripped completely naked and soaped up. By the time he had found the spot to shower, the rain had slowed. Once he was fully soaped up…the rain had all but stopped.

Ensign ended up having to use his rain-soaked towel to wipe the soap from his body. He then put half his clothes back on and walked the muddy trail back to the bathroom at the rest stop. Ensign spent the next five minutes hoping nobody walked in on him while he splashed sink water on himself; he needed to wash off the soap which the rain had failed to wash off. Ensign dressed again and walked to his car. The whole "natural shower" process took him forty-five minutes; from the time he found the path until he was back in his car...questionably cleaner than he had been before the idea crossed his chemically altered mind.

Ensign hadn't been to Minnesota. It was the first new state to cross off from his travel list. He was close to that first check mark. Ensign was on his way to stay with a transgender woman, in her apartment, in downtown Minneapolis. The two of them had been talking for a few weeks. Ensign was happy to travel to see her, but he felt a weird vibe from the beginning. Though the invitation was for an indefinite time parameter, Ensign had a feeling the visit would last no more than a day. The timeframe didn't matter. Ensign had another idea; a plan he could execute once he left the apartment.

His assumption was correct. Ensign didn't even stay at the apartment for a full twenty-four hours. The vibe was off. The lady was instantly too clingy and overbearing. When he departed, the lady gave Ensign a stun gun as a weird random departing gift. Ensign told her it was an odd thing to give him. She insisted he take it, so he did.

Back on the weekend when he moved out of his house in November of 2018, Ensign dealt with a situation which complicated his move. There was a girl who took a bus to his house, all the way from Missouri. Her name was Dana. Dana and Ensign shared a complicated four days together. Ensign had finally managed to get her onto a train to take her back to Minneapolis, where her family resided. Ensign wasn't sure what had happened in Missouri to end Dana's stay there, but she managed to get back to Minneapolis. Ensign finally focused on moving out of his house once Dana was gone.

Dana and Ensign were in contact randomly since then. Ensign knew she was no longer staying with her mom in Saint Paul, Minnesota. She was staying in a college apartment with three other roommates in downtown Minneapolis. Ensign called Dana as he drove through the city. She told him the name of the apartment where she lived. Ensign called her again when he was in the apartment lobby. Dana met him by the front desk. She ran up to him and hugged him tightly.

Ensign spent the week with Dana and her friends. Dana took him to her mom's house in Saint Paul, where he met various members of her family. Ensign ended up tattooing Dana's mom. The tattoo was of her girlfriend's name on the left side of her chest. Dana's mom told Ensign the tattoo was going to serve as a homecoming present when her girlfriend was released from prison a week later.

Ensign stayed with Dana at the downtown college apartment in Minneapolis. Dana's roommates were gone; all back in their home cities on summer break from college. Ensign stayed there with Dana, one of Dana's friends, and Dana's cousin.

Shortly after the four of them woke up one morning, one of Dana's roommates aggressively came through the front door to the fifteenth-floor apartment. Suddenly, Ensign was in the middle of a situation. He had no idea what was happening. The yelling quickly escalated to physical violence. Ensign tried his best to stay between Dana and her roommate, but many of the punches got through. In the ensuing chaos, Ensign managed to grab his belongings and remove Dana from the apartment, down the hallway, and into the elevator.

The fight resumed outside, fifteen floors below. In the courtyard outside the apartment building, security guards, Dana's friend, and Ensign did all they could to keep the two ladies separated. A car screeched to a halt on the street by the courtyard. At the same time, Dana's cousin made it down from the fifteenth floor and out into the courtyard. As Dana's cousin ran up to join in the fight, two of the roommate's friends ran up from the car in the street to join the altercation. Bystanders tried to help pull the fighting girls apart. Some of them absorbed punches from the ladies.

Sirens from the block over grew louder. Dana's friend and cousin took off for the cousin's car down the street. Ensign pulled Dana into his car. He saw the police pull up in his mirror as they swarmed the courtyard looking for the violence in the group of bystanders. Ensign was almost certain all the girls involved in the actual altercation had managed to scatter before the police caught them.

Dana was still worked up as Ensign drove from the scene. She was yelling and had tears in her eyes. Her clothes were ripped, spotted with blood, and streaked with dirt. Ensign managed to calm her down. They stopped at a gas station outside the city. On the phone, Dana's cousin told Dana that they also made it safely from the scene. They planned to meet at Dana's mom's place in Saint Paul. Ensign realized something on that drive: he not only left his newly gifted stun gun up in a bedroom of the fifteenth-floor apartment, but he left his car jump starter battery pack in the apartment as well. Ensign wasn't happy about it, but he conceded the loss.

Ensign dropped Dana off at her mom's place in Saint Paul. He left the city and drove back to Minneapolis. Ensign found a park on the west side of the city. He parked in the small parking lot next to the street and then walked down to look at the water of the pond. Ensign realized something; he quickly turned to head back. He had locked his keys in his car.

As the hot Sun beat down on him for the next half hour, Ensign did all he could to try to break into his car. He tried to use branches, rocks, and anything else he could find to wedge a gap in his window.

Ensign gave up as a pretty lady pulled up alongside his car. She had seen his failed attempts to unlock his door. She told Ensign she knew a locksmith. The lady sent the locksmith a message on her phone, and then she left. Another hour passed. Two guys in a van rolled up to Ensign's car. One of the guys got out of the van with a kit; similar to the kit the officer had used on Ensign's car back at Jane's house in Ohio. After an additional fifteen minutes, Ensign was pouring sweat back in the driver's seat of his car. He immediately drank two bottles of water. He then left the Minneapolis area. Ensign was done with the city.

Ensign pulled into a rest stop in Saint Cloud, Minnesota as the Sun completely left the sky. It was nighttime. The rest stop was extremely crowded. The commercial truck lot was full, and overflow trucks were lining the ramps connecting the rest stop to the highway. Shady characters wandered around in the lot; between the many passenger vehicles which were posted up for the night. Ensign put the shades up in the windows of his car, and he did drugs while he interacted with people on his phone. Eventually, he managed to get a few hours of sleep.

The next morning, Ensign knew he had to address an issue with his car; one which was long overdue. He drove through Saint Cloud. It was the Fourth of July. He managed to find an open auto supply store. Ensign bought new front brakes, rotors, and the correct brake fluid. He found an appropriate parking lot around mid-afternoon. The lot was empty except for the cars up front near the Walmart entrance. Ensign parked along the side of the building as far across from the pharmacy as he could. He then began to gather up the needed tools.

The next hours, into the dark of night, were spent changing the brakes and rotor for the front, driver's side wheel. Ensign could see the flashing of fireworks in the distance on the horizon. He could hear fireworks coming from multiple directions sporadically throughout the evening. Ensign completed the work on his car as the holiday ended. He was dirty, he was soaked in sweat, and he had mosquito bites. He was hot, dehydrated, and exhausted.

The sunrise was breathtaking as Ensign drove on the interstate the next morning. He set up his phone to record video as he drove west in Minnesota. Ensign's chemical enhancement had fueled his drive through the night. As the Sun rose, so did Ensign's mental state. He felt a twinge of excitement as he knew he was about to check more states off of his list. Ensign had loose plans with people all over the western half of the country. He knew that once he left Minnesota, the true adventure would begin.

When he left the Midwest, Ensign also left behind a business which he no longer wished to continue practicing. He still had a decent quantity with him, but overall, it was strictly a personal supply. Ensign got out of the game, for the most part, when he headed west into unfamiliar territory. He had planned it for a long time. He was finally able to put his plan into action. Ensign felt optimistic about the future, though he had no idea how he was going to make ends meet down the road.

That moment wasn't the time to concern himself with such matters. The stress, in that moment, had melted away.

Annapurna

It was hot and sunny when Ensign crossed from Minnesota to Fargo, North Dakota. He drove through the city until he found a rest stop. He gathered up his drugs, a towel, body wash, and a clean set of clothing. Ensign went inside and paid for a shower. The rest stop was crowded. He waited in the lounge area until his number was called. He walked down the hallway until he found the appropriate room number. Once inside, Ensign locked the door. He stripped and set up his drug tray. Ensign did a hotrail and placed his phone so he could video-call with a lady from the internet as he showered.

Truck stop/travel center showers were always enjoyable experiences. The rooms were usually quite spacious. There was a sink area, a toilet area, a bench to sit on, racks to hang clothes and towels, and a tile shower area comparable to the size of the walk-in closet in Ensign's old bedroom in Ohio. Rest stop showers were perfect spots to take breaks from driving, get clean, do drugs, use the facilities, and video-interact with others in privacy.

Forty-five minutes later, Ensign was back outside at his car. He was pouring sweat again as soon as he stepped outside the service center. Ensign decided to spend the day in Fargo working on more of his car audio system. Between his meth consumption and his compulsive purchases of stereo components, his work was never done. Ensign traveled with all the needed tools in his car. Anywhere became a good spot to add more sound to his Lexus.

Hours later, Ensign was driving on the interstate, heading

south in the Dakotas. He saw something on that stretch of highway which he had never before seen. The speed limit signs: they all were posted for eighty miles per hour. There were spots in Michigan posted at seventy-five. Those Dakota speed limit signs became the fastest posted speeds he had ever seen. Ensign made sure to record video as he sped by the signs.

Ensign was going to be passing through Sioux Falls, South Dakota later on that day. He had been messaging back-and-forth with an Asian lady who was a resident in that city. According to her, she was recently divorced, and she had moved into a hotel room with her dog and all her belongings. She wanted Ensign to stop to see her on his way through the city. Ensign agreed. The lady sent him an address, and Ensign replied to her with the ETA.

Though he hadn't been paying attention to the coronavirus pandemic as he traveled the country in 2020, Ensign was reminded it existed when he stopped at a gas station in South Dakota. He walked down an aisle in the store as he looked for antibiotic ointment. (He used the ointment as he perpetually tattooed himself, and his supply had run out.) Ensign scrunched up his face in disbelief as he noticed half of a particular aisle of the store was stocked with nothing but four-ounce bottles of hand sanitizer. Each bottle had a price tag. Each four-ounce bottle was being sold for eight dollars and ninety-five cents.

Ensign shook his head as he decided he wasn't going to give any of his money to that particular establishment. As he began to walk to the door, the store clerk came out from a back room. He looked at Ensign and instantly began to speak.

"Sir, you MUST have on a mask to be inside this store."

Ensign looked him in the eyes. He then spoke one word with emphasis to let him know his thoughts of the demand.

"Ha!"

Ensign opened the door and walked outside in disgust. He decided he wasn't going to make any more stops until he made it to the Asian lady's hotel. Two hours later, he reached the exit in Sioux Falls. Ensign could see the hotel from the interstate exit. It was off of a service drive, adjacent to two other hotels.

Ensign knocked on the door to the hotel room. The lady opened the door and led him inside by his hand. She then kissed him and told him to get comfortable on the bed. She went into the bathroom and shut the door. Ensign sat back against the headboard of the bed in the hotel room. He took note of the many racks of hanging clothes filling up the far side of the room. Ensign could tell that the lady had moved all of her belongings into her small hotel room. Her dog lay on the floor in a dog bed over by the window.

Twenty minutes passed. Ensign walked to the bathroom door and knocked. He asked if the lady was alright. She responded that she was. Ensign sat back down. Ten more minutes passed. The lady finally stepped out of the bathroom. She told Ensign to come outside with her as she walked her dog.

The two of them walked down to the end of the hallway, and they stepped out to the side of the hotel. The lady told Ensign she was going to smoke a cigarette. Ensign told her he was going to walk around to his car in the parking lot on the other side of the building.

Once in his car, Ensign put the shades up in his windows. He injected crystal into his arm. Ensign sat for a bit while the drugs hit and washed over him. He sat a bit longer. He decided something after another ten minutes passed. He wasn't going to go back to the lady's hotel room. She hadn't texted him to come back inside, and he hadn't texted her to say he wasn't coming back. Ensign pushed the button to start his car, and he left Sioux Falls, South Dakota.

Urine Sane

It was a long drive through the Dakotas; two more states crossed off the list. Ensign reached Iowa. Iowa was not new to him. Ensign used to have a job site in Iowa; back when he still had a career. He used to take his company car to his job site in Iowa. One time, as he was traveling with the operations manager who worked underneath him, they became stranded in Iowa. Ensign had fueled his car at a gas station; a gas station which somehow had water in their fuel pumps. Ensign's car broke down on a bridge over the Mississippi river. That was back in 2013.

In 2020, Ensign was on the opposite side of the state. He reached Sioux City, Iowa and began receiving online notifications from interested people on the border of Iowa and Nebraska. It was early morning. The Sun hadn't yet risen. Ensign opened a message from a guy who had just finished his shift at the slaughterhouse in South Sioux City, Nebraska. Ensign told him he would be at his house by seven o'clock that morning. That meant he had only an hour before he would cross yet another state off of his travel list.

The morning sky was beginning to brighten that Friday when Ensign reached Cliff's house. The house was one block from the slaughterhouse where Cliff worked the third shift. Cliff was off work for the weekend. He partied. Cliff had a bag of his own when Ensign showed up. He wanted Ensign to try it. Cliff loaded an oil-burner stem. Ensign hit the pipe. He shook his head as he blew out a cloud. It tasted impure compared to the ounce of ice Ensign had in his pocket. Ensign flicked a crystal to Cliff, and he told him to try it.

As Cliff blew out his cloud of smoke, he instantly became animated and hyper. He had never smoked anything close to what Ensign had with him. Cliff instantly wanted to buy half an ounce from Ensign. Ensign told Cliff he was out of the game. The bags he had with him were for personal use. Ensign told him the best he could do for him was a teener. Cliff happily paid an exorbitant rate for a sixteenth of that ounce.

Between making videos and doing drugs, Cliff took Ensign around the city. They went to eat at a few local favorite restaurants. They got groceries at the store to grill out in Cliff's backyard. At one point, Cliff went to a cookout at his sister's house. During that time, Ensign went to meet up with a guy named Noah who had found him on one of the apps.

Noah was twenty-four years old. Ensign picked him up from his house in Iowa. Noah didn't do drugs, but he didn't mind Ensign doing them in his presence. Had Noah been concerned with it; Ensign would have waited to do drugs until after he dropped Noah back off at his house that evening.

Noah directed Ensign to a park he liked to hike. Ensign was amazed that there was a hill in Iowa which could almost have been mistaken for a mountain. They drove up the winding road to the top of the hill. Ensign parked along the side of the road by the scenic overlook at the summit. They hiked through the trees on the top of the hill.

Noah, same as Jerry in Lansing, had an unrealized fantasy of being peed on. Ensign had an idea for an interesting video while he was in the park with Noah. Ensign framed the camera angle prior to recording the video. He climbed up a tree across from where he set up the camera. Ensign was about eight feet up in the air as Noah was naked on his knees on the ground. Ensign peed from up in the tree...all over Noah.

Ensign stopped at a rest stop so Noah could go wash up in the bathroom. Ensign did drugs and edited the video while Noah was inside. When he dropped Noah back at his house, Noah thanked him for coming to see him. Noah had Ensign promise to send him the finished video. Later that night, back at Cliff's house in Nebraska, Ensign remembered to send Noah the video. Noah thanked Ensign in a text.

Heyoka

Maps of the United States can be easily misleading. The states in the western half of the country are all much larger than most of the eastern states. On maps, since the reference point for the size of those western states is other adjacent western states, misconstrued assumptions of distance and travel time go unrealized until actually driving through the western half of the country.

In the eastern half of the country, multiple states are easily fully crossed, from one side to the other, within a single day of driving. The states out West are different. It becomes a different feeling when hours and hours of driving still don't result in reaching the halfway point of a single state. The excitement of crossing new state borders isn't applicable in single days of travel out West. It becomes demotivational knowing that the day will end in the same state it began.

Driving west in Nebraska became Ensign's first acknowledgement of that line of thought. He left Cliff's house in South Sioux City, Nebraska. Ensign wasn't able to set a goal to make it through to the next state by the end of the same day. He just faced the situation and drove. As hours passed, he kept plugging along. The low rolling hills and farmland were perpetual peripheral scenery. The Sun shone bright to the green and golden-brown land of Nebraska as Ensign kept on driving west.

Morning passed into afternoon. Afternoon became evening. The hours became difficult when the evening Sun was directly in front of Ensign. Later on, as evening gave way to night, Ensign was able to see again as he drove without the Sun shining through his front windshield. The traffic on the Nebraska highway was minimal. Ensign had clear vision in front of him. He had a long way to drive to reach the other side of the state. Ensign blew down a hotrail and decided to spike his adrenaline by pressing his foot on the gas pedal of his car.

Ensign seized the opportunity. He thought back to the times on the interstates around Detroit, his own personal speedway. Ensign cranked up the music. The bass vibrated his mirrors and his seat. He felt each note reverberate through his entire body. Ensign gripped the steering wheel in front of him, and he pushed down on the gas.

The fields on either side of the road began to pass by more quickly. Ensign's focus, fueled by the drugs, became clearer. As the needle on his speedometer crossed over into triple digits, a smile crept onto his face. Ensign's foot pushed further down to the floor. He felt the power of his Lexus's engine. One twenty… one thirty…one thirty-five…He was floating.

Over the next couple of hours, Ensign balanced his legal speed-limit driving with bursts and extended stretches of pushing close to one hundred and forty miles-per-hour. Ensign wasn't going to reach the next state that particular day, but he was going to find out how close he could get.

He eventually pulled into a rest stop off the highway. Ensign talked on the phone with Luke. Luke told Ensign a crazy story about something that happened to him in Lansing that afternoon. Jerry called Ensign a few minutes after he hung up with Luke. Jerry told Ensign something else which happened to him in Lansing a few days prior. Ensign hung up the phone after that second call. Ensign considered both of those phone calls. He had been reassured he had made the right decision, leaving Lansing.

Ensign set up for the night in his car at that rest stop next to the highway in western Nebraska. The weather changed as he did hotrails and interacted online. The wind picked up almost instantly at one point. The air felt different. Ensign took the shade off his driver's side window. To the distance west of him, over the trees outlining the parking lot, lightning lit up the sky. It wasn't just a little lightning; it was nonstop. The sky was lit more than it was dark. Flashes overlapped and outshined previous lightning. He'd never seen anything like it. Ensign recorded a video for one minute for a social media site...and then the rain began. It was sporadic at first. The drops were foreboding. Ensign knew something bad was about to happen.

Ensign got back in his car and closed up the window with the shade. After he posted the video on the website, he went online to check for news bulletins. Ensign figured out his location, and he checked the internet. He pulled up radar of the sky. His eyes opened wide. Ensign found a warning from the National Weather Service.

Growing up in the Midwest, tornado warnings and severe storm warnings were common. Ensign wanted to be a storm chaser back when he was a child. He studied weather. He saw his first tornado when he was twelve years old. Ensign loved severe weather, and he was always someone who chose to run towards a storm when there was a warning to take shelter.

The storm that night in Nebraska was different. Ensign didn't have an option to shelter. He was in his car...and the warning from the National Weather Service was like no other he had ever seen. The warning wasn't written as an option or a suggestion. It was urgent, to the point, and serious. Eighty-five mile an hour wind gusts, baseball sized hail, torrential rains...destruction. Immediately, no exceptions, take cover. People and animals outside WILL be hurt...or worse.

And then...the sound...Ensign heard it start at the far west side of the parking lot. He was parked in the northeast corner. The sound got louder as it got closer. It wasn't a tornado. It was wind-driven rain and hail. The wind hit his car in bursts as he felt the car's frame swaying on the suspension. Ensign took the shade out of the passenger window. Sheets of water blotted out the giant lights on telephone poles throughout the parking lot... then, all the lights cut off. The sound of the rain and hail was as loud as the darkness was black. He was in it, and he made a choice in that moment.

Ensign turned on his car, and he very slowly drove back to the highway. He felt he was safer on the road; no longer waiting for a tree to fall on his car. The drive was slow as the rain came down; unrelentingly. After an hour, Ensign made it to the next rest stop. He hadn't slept in days. He could barely see the road in front of him. Ensign pulled into that next rest stop's parking lot...and he slept in his car.

When he was awakened by noises the next morning, Ensign saw the sunlight shining through the edges of the shades in his car windows. He pulled down the corner of the shade on his windshield; his jaw dropped. The noises had been coming from a crew of workers using power saws and woodchippers all around Ensign in the parking lot.

More than half of the trees at the rest stop had snapped at their trunks and lay in the parking lot on the ground. A mature maple tree had fallen and filled the parking space two spaces down from where Ensign had fallen asleep in his car. Trees were down behind him, in front of him, and on both sides. Ensign recorded another video. He fixed the shade to cover the windshield once more. Ensign did a hotrail.

Ensign dressed and removed the shades from all his car's windows. The workers were still sawing away at the branches of the felled trees. Ensign dodged the branches and trees which littered the pavement as he made his way back to the highway. It was a new day; sunny and cloudless. Ensign was able to set the goal to reach the border of Nebraska that day. He was only a few hours away from crossing over into Colorado for the first time in his life. Ensign was excited...and he blew down another hotrail to celebrate. He picked up speed, traveling west on the interstate.

The Golden State...Ensign saw it, beginning in western Nebraska. The rolling hills of western Nebraska were a uniform color of golden beauty. Ensign was an hour out, and he exited the highway to get food and gas. It was noon. Ensign had been driving all morning. The downed trees at the rest stop were hours behind him in his rearview mirror. Anticipation tingled in his brain, enhanced with the crystal.

It was an unfamiliar environment to him, and Ensign loved the new life experience. He knew that day that he was exactly where he was meant to be. All the choices which led him to that exact location in that specific moment in time, all the choices he didn't make…everything; it was the feeling he had been chasing for as long as he could remember. Ensign was living life. He felt it; he felt alive.

As Ensign crossed the Nebraska/Colorado border, he felt his eyes begin to mist up. He saw the world's beauty all around him and in front of him. Ensign was in a moment, a golden moment; accentuated by the color of the land all around. Ensign was significant; if only to himself. He was a passenger on a journey beyond that which he saw through his windshield. The past was behind him. The future was unknown. He was exactly where he was meant to be in all possible ways. Life made sense.

Strap In, Hold On, and Enjoy the Ride

The drive west across eastern Colorado was a mix of various levels of reality. The scenery was foreign, but Ensign knew the view from his dreams. He saw miles to the horizon in all directions. The air was hazy, which lent a mystical quality to Ensign's golden world. He experienced the drive in an extremely chemically altered consciousness. Anticipation grew with each mile.

Ensign's eyes strained to focus through the haze in front of him to the horizon; knowing he was guaranteed to see the Colorado Rocky Mountains for the first time. He didn't know how much longer he had until shocking contrast on the horizon ahead would bestow a view of snowcapped peaks, thousands of feet above the golden land. The thought excited him as he pushed forward. He was happy.

The interstate highway wound into the state and towards the Rockies. Ensign knew that as fact. As he curved around with the road, he thought he saw something in the sky, through the haze, in the distance. The highway curved back the other way. Were the drugs mixing with his anticipation and causing him to hallucinate? Ensign wasn't sure. He kept driving. He kept looking ahead to the distance…and then, he was sure. There, through the haze, he saw, with certainty, a group of mountains ahead of him; they reached into the sky above the horizon. The gray rock faces were topped with the white of snow.

Ensign turned again with the road, and they were gone. Suddenly, off to the side of his focus, another section of mountains appeared through the haze of the sky. Then more appeared in front of him. He could see the wall of ridges; suddenly filling up the full expanse of the horizon in all directions west of his current location. Ensign was heading towards a vast range of mountains stretching as far north and south as he could see. He had been driving across the entire country, and the ground had been basically flat during those weeks he had been driving. Everything changed in that moment, a new experience with a completely different feel. Ensign loved everything in that moment.

Ensign reached Denver in late afternoon. He kept driving west. He went, with the road, up into the mountains. It was rush hour, and the mountain highway was congested with vehicles. Ensign stopped at various spots amongst the mountains as he recorded videos. He sent clips to his friends as he drove through the mountains, west of Denver. Ensign made a decision as he was stopped at a scenic overlook above the city. He would come back to Denver another day. He wanted to check off another state from his travel list by day's end. Ensign decided to double back east a couple of miles to meet up with the interstate running north and south in Denver. Ensign knew he could make it to Wyoming if he got back on the road.

...

The next morning, he jolted awake in his car. Ensign gathered his bearings about him as he put on his glasses. The yelling, which woke him up, continued. Though the screaming and shouting was close enough to make out the words, the words made no sense. Ensign pulled out his tray and torch. He did a hotrail. He then removed the shades from his car windows.

It was sunny outside. Ensign's eyes took a second to adjust. He stepped from his car. He was then standing in the parking lot of a rest stop between the Colorado/Wyoming border and Cheyanne, Wyoming. Ensign had reached his goal of making it to Wyoming in the middle of the night. He felt rested after the couple of hours of car sleep. He looked around to where he heard the screaming. Ensign saw where it was coming from…and from whom.

Ensign made eye contact with a vagrant, standing between the parking lot and the road. He was about a hundred yards from Ensign; at the base of the sign for the travel center. Ensign turned away to walk through the parking lot; into the rest stop to use the bathroom. The vagrant picked up ranting, right where he had left off.

"...and AMERICA! No, they won't go! NO! God blessed this land..."

When Ensign walked back out to his car, a police officer was trying to reason with the guy's nonsense. It wasn't working. Eventually, as Ensign prepared to leave the rest stop, the officer must have reached his limit in patience. He didn't arrest the vagrant. Instead, he stepped back in his patrol car and drove away. Ensign thought to himself; he would have done the exact same thing in the officer's situation. Ensign started his car. He followed the officer out of the rest stop on his way back to the highway.

Ensign reached Cheyanne, Wyoming. He explored the city. He ate at a Mexican restaurant. He recorded videos and interacted with people online. Ensign found a park in the middle of the city. He spent a few hours rewiring the two twelve-inch subwoofers in the trunk of his car. When he finished, Ensign put his tools away and began work on another project.

The Dude Abides

In 2016, Ensign stopped drinking alcohol. He was getting used to sobriety. Ensign was pleasantly surprised, no longer depending on alcohol to get through his days. Sobriety allowed him to focus more on other aspects of his life. He was also newly living alone in his house in Ohio. Ensign's marriage ended earlier that year. Loneliness; an ironic constant companion.

Ensign knew he wasn't ready for a sincere relationship, but female companionship still played a role in his life. 2016 was the time when Ensign began developing dynamics to fill a void he had felt for a long time. Though his marriage had completely ended in 2016, Ensign's loneliness had been consistently present a long time prior to the end of his marriage. A large part of why his marriage ended was due to his inability to process and share his feelings. Long before his marriage ended, Ensign had closed off emotionally.

As with his other serious relationships prior, the beginning period of Ensign's marriage was amazing. He shared himself. He was happy. It was new and exciting in the beginning. Ensign didn't have time to focus on his own unhappiness when he was distracted by a new dynamic with an amazing woman. As with his previous relationships, reality crept in over time. Ensign lost focus on positivity. He regressed into a self-absorbed and closed-off world; expecting happiness to occur without applying any real effort to ensure it happened.

At the end of 2016, Ensign was floating in the abyss. His dynamics with women began the process of forgetting himself all over again while interacting in new "relationships" on various levels of shared intimacy. Ensign was trying to fill a void as he was trying to find himself in a new sober and single world. He picked up with previous dynamics, he forged new connections, and he took intimacy as it came to him; on whatever levels he connected.

There was a girl Ensign had known in passing since he was a child in elementary school. Though a grade ahead of him, she went to the same school through all of Ensign's school years. During his elementary school days, Ensign's mom taught "CCD" on Tuesday nights at their city's catholic church. CCD, or Confraternity of Catholic Doctrine, was a class which taught religion to public school children. Shannon happened to be one of his mom's students, back when they were in elementary school.

Though Shannon and Ensign didn't associate during their time from elementary school through high school, they randomly crossed paths at parties and other events. Later on, they were connected via social media as they periodically interacted in the real world, at bars and social functions. By the end of 2016, when Ensign was single for the first extended time period in his adult life, Shannon and Ensign began consistently interacting with one another.

Their dynamic blossomed quickly and organically. Ensign shared everything with Shannon. The more he shared, the deeper he felt the connection. The more something became an experience just for the two of them...the more the moment became exclusively theirs, the more invested he became...the more Ensign was aroused and into it.

Shannon gave Ensign instructions to please her. She told him what to do in videos for her. When Ensign sent her the videos, she gave him feedback. Their dynamic grew more intimate with each task and video he completed for her. Their relationship set the groundwork for Ensign's online interactions when he joined the website, over a year later.

Their dynamic remained a constant in Ensign's life as time passed. The dynamic grew as life became something entirely new to him. When Ensign stepped from all familiarity and began his foray into a strange and foreign existence, Shannon's presence in his life remained one of the very few dependable focuses he was able to maintain.

...

Ensign smiled as he read the text message. He had spent the afternoon working hard on his car audio system. Ensign was glad to be relaxing in his driver's seat at the rest stop; after leaving Cheyanne, Wyoming. The text message was the same two words Shannon had sent an hour prior, when he was finishing the car audio work in Cheyanne. Shannon gave Ensign a reprieve, that hour, while he drove west. When Ensign let her know that he had made it to a rest stop west of the city, Shannon texted him those same two words again.

"Do it."

Ensign replied an affirmative as he retrieved his equipment from a bag in the back of his car. He had previously modified one of his tattoo machines. Ensign had wired the cord from the foot pedal to a trigger switch on the handle of the machine. He also replaced the plug to the power unit with a USB attachment. Ensign was fully able to hook the machine to his car, or a battery pack, and operate the machine while he was seated in his driver's seat. Ensign received another two-word text message from Shannon.

"Video it."

Ensign sent videos as he followed Shannon's directions. A half hour later, he sent the final video update. Ensign put some thought into the cinematography of that final recording. The Sun was setting. It was beautiful; looking out over the rest stop parking lot to the colorful sky as the light began to fade in the valley below. Ensign began the recording with a steady framing of the Sun as it set over the mountains in the distance to the West. He panned the camera to show a panoramic view of the sky's colors above the Wyoming valley. At the end of the scenic recording, the camera view reached the side of the passenger window on the inside of Ensign's car. He then panned immediately down to his lap. There, the camera focused on the green lightning bolt, complete with a black outline, on his right ball.

Ensign put antibiotic ointment on the new tattoo, and he zipped up his pants. The video was well-received. Not just by Shannon, but by the select few others with whom he chose to share that moment. Ensign sat at the rest stop and thought for a few minutes on something else. He then acted on the thoughts.

Ensign went online and searched to find reviews of the best rotary tattoo machine available for purchase. He read multiple reviews. He found the proper website to make the purchase. Ensign threw himself a curveball as he purchased the tattoo machine.

Though he was currently in Wyoming; heading west, Ensign chose to have the expensive tattoo machine shipped to a locker at a grocery store in the center of Santa Fe, New Mexico. Ensign was doing all he could to check off all the states on his travel list. New Mexico was out of his way the other direction. Ensign created a reason to travel to New Mexico.

He set the delivery date for a week and a half later. Ensign had time to visit Yellowstone. He had time to stop and see people as he traveled south through Colorado on his return from Wyoming. When he ordered the tattoo machine, he created a plan. He was going to check New Mexico off of his travel list for sure. Ensign had created a new quest; he had a mission, and a timeline to fulfill the mission.

The Ones and Twos

Ensign pushed westward through the evening and into the darkness of night. Wyoming was vast and barren with windswept hills and lonely clusters of mountains. Drugs ran their course, and Ensign felt an urge to sleep.

There was an exit from the highway. It curved around and steeply up into a mountain pass. There was a small service station on the right side of the road up in the mountains. Everything was black in all other directions.

Ensign pulled into the gas station parking lot. He sat in his car for a moment as he took stock of his immediate surroundings. There were a couple of other cars in parking spaces up closer to the store's entrance. Someone seated in one of the cars stared at Ensign while he surveyed the area. Someone else inside the store walked to the front and stared at him through the glass store window. A small alarm bell went off in the back of Ensign's mind. He felt an urgent need to immediately leave the parking lot.

Ensign hopped back on the road and headed further away from the highway. He checked his mirrors; nobody had pulled out to follow him. Ensign's music was off, and he heard a low rumbling from the dark section of road to his left, down a small slope. He looked over. Ensign did a double take. He'd never seen anything like it.

Twenty years in the transportation and logistics industry, and Ensign was still shocked. The sheer number: like nothing he'd ever seen outside of the largest distribution centers and most massive drop lots around the country. There were hundreds of semitrucks to his left. Some with their running lights marking their outlines, others completely blacked out alongside them. It was too dark outside to see how far along the trucks continued. Ensign could see truck lights in at least five rows of depth away from the highway.

Though apprehensive, Ensign was intrigued. He was also tired. Ensign pulled off the road to the left, and down into the roadside corral of stationary tractor-trailers. He drove into the lines of massive idling machines. The noise of the countless idling engines vibrated Ensign's car in the absence of his music. He meandered back in the direction of where he left that service station. Ensign weaved his way back as he cut deeper through the lines of trucks parked farther from the hill up to the road.

Ensign parked in the fourth row deep, and he turned off all but his running lights. He didn't want to be conspicuous, but he also didn't want a truck to flatten him; pulling through his parking location to rest alongside the other semis. Ensign's small black sports car, with blacked out windows, wouldn't have stood a chance if a truck driver hadn't seen him until it was too late.

Ensign sat for a minute amongst the sea of giant machines and their cargo. He again evaluated his current situation in that moment. Ensign decided he was safe where he was. He put the shades up in his windows, he pulled out his drug supplies, he did drugs, and he stripped naked after he did drugs. Ensign interacted on his phone with people from the internet.

Ensign suddenly awoke to daylight shining brightly, filling his car with the morning. He was still naked. The shade which had been in his windshield had fallen from its place, and it was on the passenger-side floor. Maybe the trucks around him had vibrated it loose. Ensign instantly put the shade back in place and dressed, as he embarrassingly woke up fully unclothed in that weird field of trucks.

Most of the trucks from the previous night were no longer parked there. Ensign saw about twenty trucks still scattered around his immediate location. He kicked up dust as he hurried up and drove through the lot to an entranceway, back to the main road on the side of the hill. Ensign wondered how many of the trucks had passed by the front of his car as they vacated the lot to return to driving to their destinations. Their views, looking down into his windshield as they passed him by, would have been fully unobstructed. They would have seen a heavily tattooed and fully naked sleeper in the midst of a midlife crisis adventure.

Ensign's car seemed to drive funny once he was back on the road. It pulled to the right. The drive was bumpier than normal. It felt better once he got up to highway speed. The outside air grew hotter that morning at a rapid rate. Ensign could tell the temperature was already in the predicted high nineties. He drove for another hour. Ensign did not have any water left in his car. He was also getting hungry. He had no food.

It happened in an instant. The sound, the smell, the feel. Ensign knew exactly what had happened. The sound: a mix between a pop and a rip. The smell: smoke and burning chemicals. The feeling: an instant pull on his steering wheel as his car vibrated like it was about to fall apart. Ensign's speed dropped from eighty-five to about fifty very quickly. In his mirrors, he saw smoke trailing his car. Ensign maintained control of the wheel as he let his car decelerate on its own terms. He didn't touch the brakes until he dropped below twenty miles an hour and found a good section of shoulder; one which to pull off and have clearance from the right travel lane of the highway.

Ensign stepped out of his car. The back passenger-side tire was shredded the entire way around the wheel hub. Smoke was still coming out from the wheel as his car sat directly on the rim. Ensign had his spare tire with him, so he went to work locating the proper socket to remove the lug nuts and change the tire.

An hour passed in that awful heat, and Ensign wasn't having any luck finding the socket. He had already sheltered twice in his car as random isolated storms ripped through the area. Ensign had been driving through those random, single-cloud, mini-severe, thunderstorms all morning. Though each storm only lasted a couple minutes, they proved to be an inconvenience while Ensign was searching for the tools to begin repairs.

After that first hour, a dreadful thought crossed Ensign's mind. He remembered leaving a specific bag of tools back at his storage unit in Ohio. He knew he was going to be driving thousands of miles, so he wanted to lighten the weight of his car in any way possible. Ensign remembered that the specific socket, the one which fit his lug nuts, was in that bag of tools back at his storage unit. His heart sank.

It had been two hours since Ensign finished the last of the water with him in his car when he woke up in that field of trucks that morning. It was ninety-five degrees outside. Those wayward isolated superstorms did nothing to cool off the air. Ensign hadn't seen a single car pass by him on the highway the entire time he had been looking for his tools. He was thirsty. He was worried. He was in the most desolate and isolated physical location he had ever been. The weather was extreme. Ensign's supplies were depleted...and his phone had absolutely zero reception.

The windswept landscape on both sides of the highway in all directions was dusty, rocky, and empty. Ensign took his phone from the seat of his car and crossed over the picket fence on the north side of the highway. It took him about ten minutes to get to the very top of the hill. Ensign could see for miles in all directions from the top of the hill. All he saw looked the exact same. It was barren and dusty. Hills popped up across the landscape at random points. He saw no cars on the road, stretching to both sides of the horizon. Ensign's phone still had no reception.

From that vantage point atop the hill, Ensign saw another storm in the distance. An isolated cloud formation was moving at him fast. He recorded video of the scene as he began to quickly descend the hill to reach his car to take shelter. Ensign made it back just as the stormfront hit. Two minutes later, the storm had passed. Ensign's car, and the road, began to dry instantly in the heat.

Ensign sat, sweating in his car, for the next five hours. As storms rolled through, he had to keep all of his windows up. Ensign may as well have just stood on the road in the rain. He was as soaked from sweat as he would have been had he been outside his car in the rain. Finally, as if a miracle, a car pulled up and parked behind him. Ensign sat up in disbelief. Instantly, he jumped from his car. The police cruiser door opened, and an officer stepped out to meet him on the side of the road.

"Oh, my God! I'm so happy to see you. I've been here six hours without water. I can't believe another car finally came down this road."

The officer came upon Ensign on a routine drive down the highway. He had water with him in his cruiser. He gave Ensign six bottles to drink. Ensign downed the first three in under a minute. The officer handed Ensign a box of crackers. Ensign ate half of them as they talked. The officer also had one more item which made him Ensign's hero; he had a tire iron. The officer changed Ensign's tire to the spare. He insisted Ensign just sat back while he did the work. That officer, on that day, was genuinely Ensign's hero.

The officer looked up the closest places with tire shops from where Ensign was stopped on the side of the road. Ensign had the option to drive one hundred miles back in the opposite direction. He had another option as well; he could drive two hundred miles farther west, the direction he had been traveling...on the spare donut tire from his trunk.

Ensign chose option number two. He decided to keep heading west. He thanked the officer sincerely for saving him that day. He then drove two hundred miles through Wyoming at eighty miles per hour on a donut. Ensign made it to the tire store in that next city...and they didn't have a tire to fit his Lexus.

The tire store employee called ahead to another tire shop in Rock Springs, Wyoming. They had the proper sized tires to fit his car in Rock Springs. Rock Springs was yet another hundred miles west on the same highway; the road where Ensign had already put two hundred miles on the donut. He didn't have a choice.

Ensign got back on the road, crossed his fingers, and he pushed down the gas pedal one more time.

Ensign made it to Rock Springs. He found the tire store. They had one barely used tire that fit his car. They only charged Ensign thirty-five dollars for the tire. Ensign left the waiting room of the extremely large tire store within an hour. He had done his day's driving. He decided to post up in Rock Springs, cruise around and check out the city, and see who from the online world was close to him.

Ensign tattooed himself as he sat; parked at a rest stop overnight in Rock Springs. He interacted with online friends and did drugs. Ensign stayed awake that whole night. Before the Sun came up the next morning, he made a decision. Ensign went into the travel center and bought a shower. He was excited as he gathered up his belongings after he showered. Ensign walked back to his car. He put directions into his GPS for Yellowstone.

Chirality

Ensign's excitement to explore new frontiers caused him to leave the rest stop in haste. He drove an hour north from Rock Springs and pulled his car into a gas station. The gas station was closed for another hour. Ensign parked at the pump and waited. The Sun came up as he waited to fuel. Ensign didn't mind the wait. His anticipation had him feeling wonderful...and the drugs he did in his car helped him pass the time.

As with his first trip into Colorado earlier in the week, Ensign looked for the mountains as he drove north towards Yellowstone. The farther north he drove, the more mountains appeared on the horizon. Ensign reached Jackson, Wyoming in early afternoon. He felt he had entered through the gates of an enchanted world of fantasy. He was no longer on flat ground. Ensign could no longer see for miles to a horizon in all directions. He was in a special place; the majesty of nature surrounded him.

The natural beauty of Hawaii had mesmerized him years prior. Ensign felt fortunate any time he took trips to the Caribbean on other occasions. He found beauty everywhere in the continental United States during his travels throughout his life, especially in his recent years of wanderlust. Nature had fostered and cultivated a wonderful part of his psyche since he was old enough to first make memories. It was that day when nature humbled Ensign as he had never before been. That day for Ensign, as he drove north from Jackson, Wyoming to Jackson Hole, was a game changer. That day...Ensign's mind was blown.

Ensign was thankful for everything in those ten meditative

hours he spent at Teton Point Turnout. All of everything made sense. Those ten hours stretched with him on to eternity. He was nothing without all else, and nothing was everything...it all was, is, and would be ever after.

On that day, in that location, Ensign felt something beyond what words could explain. Ensign knew everything was ok... no matter what, in all situations, at all times, with all things... it was all ok. Ensign never feared death as an adult. At times, he sought it out or wished for it...but in that moment, in that location, on that day...he let go of his fear of living. He let go of everything, and as he did, he feared nothing at all.

That moment, as Ensign bathed in the splendor of the Teton Mountains, in the field at the base of Grand Teton...he transcended. All which had happened to that point, all which had not...all over which he had control, all of which he did not... it all ended in the shadow of the Teton Mountains on that day in the summer of 2020. It all ceased to exist, and Ensign stepped through. He stepped through; to all beyond. As he stepped through, Ensign felt it, and he knew it. It was electric. It was perfect. It was always there for him, and it would always remain. Ensign's perspective, on that day, shifted to that which lay in wait of his arrival.

As that so-important day came to a close, and as Ensign continued his drive north from Jackson Hole, Wyoming...it all made sense. He was ok...everything was ok. Ensign knew he could have died in that moment, and all would have been right. He knew he could die at any point beyond, and all would be ok. He knew he could live, and anything at all could happen while alive, and all would be as it was meant to be. That moment split Ensign's life in two; all which came before, and all which would come after. In the shadow of those majestic mountains, as he sat there...Ensign knew the moment had changed him forever.

Layers

Ensign woke up in his car. He could see the morning sunlight through the cracks around the shades in his windows. He thought for a moment to try to sort out where he was waking up. Ensign remembered driving through an open and large wooden gate at around three o'clock in the morning. He remembered, though the road had been black except for in front of him where his headlights had been shining, he was on the edge of a drop off. There was a guardrail to his right side where he parked. The small section of gravel between the road and the guardrail had been large enough to exactly fit his car. Ensign had parked under a metal sign which warned of the presence of bears in the area.

Ensign could hear traffic zipping by his car to the left of him. He kept the shades on the windows of the driver's side and rear windshield. Ensign removed the shades from the front windshield and the passenger side of his car. Sun instantly filled his car with light. The smoke from the hotrail was sparkling in the air. The sign, which warned of bears, was ahead of him, posted five feet above his car on a tree.

When he looked out the windows on the right side of his car, all Ensign saw was sky. He leaned over to climb into the passenger seat. Ensign still only saw sky...until he put his head up to the passenger window. He saw where he had parked and slept. Ensign had parked on the very apex of an eight-hundred-foot sheer cliff drop-off. He had slept inches from a cliff; one which rivaled the proverbial cliff of his midlife crisis. He cracked the passenger door to look down.

There was four inches of pavement between his car and the

drop. It was just enough room for the guard rail to be cemented there in place...and it was as far as he could open his car door before he hit it on the rail. Ensign got out of his car on the driver's side. He waited by the guardrail until traffic passed and he didn't hear any more cars approaching. Ensign then peed off the apex of an eight-hundred-foot sheer cliff drop-off. He was a homeless person doing homeless activities.

Prioritizing

Ensign had been in Yellowstone since he passed through the large open wooden gate at three o'clock in the morning. Ensign stopped at canyons, overlooking rivers of rapids hundreds of feet below. He stopped to record video at a pristine lake. He hiked around waterfalls. Ensign had to slow down as he drove. He was behind a couple of cars full of passengers recording videos of bison sleeping on the roadside. Ensign recorded videos as well.

He located Old Faithful on the map. Ensign parked in the extremely large and crowded parking lot. There were hundreds of people everywhere. Ensign walked around and checked out the scenery. Ensign took a seat with the hundreds of people waiting for the next eruption. The schedule was posted on the large wooden observation deck.

After ten minutes of waiting as the time approached, Ensign began recording video. For the next six minutes and fifteen seconds, he recorded Old Faithful shooting hot water from the hole in the ground. It was yet another video he added to his collection...a collection which included a video a girl had requested earlier that day; one of him stripping as a river in Yellowstone flowed past him.

At one point, Ensign crossed the Continental Divide. He stopped at an overlook high up in the mountains of Yellowstone. He could see miles in front of him from the top of the mountain. The Rocky Mountains in Yellowstone had lived up to all he had hoped. He stopped again after he drove down and out of the park. Ensign recorded video of the sunset over the Tetons from the shore of Jackson Lake. In the day and a half, in that magical corner of northwest Wyoming, Ensign saw and documented some of the most beautiful natural settings he had ever seen. Ensign's choice to drive north from Rock Springs had changed his life.

It was dark outside when Ensign stopped at a busy gas station in the center of Jackson, Wyoming. He was on his way back to Rock Springs. Ensign knew he wasn't going to make the full drive back down the western side of Wyoming that night. He decided to drive as far as he could before he stopped for sleep.

Ensign pulled into a gas station somewhere in the middle of the state. He paid for gas. Ensign put the nozzle in his car's gas tank. He sat down in his car as it began to fuel. Ensign woke up to a police officer tapping on his window. Two hours had passed. The employee at the gas station, instead of attempting to wake him, had called the police.

Ensign explained to the officer where he was going, and from where he had been driving. The officer told Ensign of a nearby street with open parking. Ensign found the location and pulled in between two other parked vehicles. He slept for three more hours. Ensign left for Rock Springs as the Sun came up the next morning.

The Coriolis Effect

His phone rang as Ensign did laundry at a laundromat in Rock Springs, Wyoming. Though he had just hung up with her, Allison was calling him back. Ensign stepped outside to the street to answer his phone.

"Hi, again…"

"I'll be back from the boat earlier today than I told you a minute ago. I want to see you. Can I see you?"

"Absolutely. my laundry is almost done. I'm about to go wash my car. Give me a call once you get back from the water. I'll let you know where I'm at later on."

"I'm excited to see you."

"I'm excited to see you, too."

"Bye, Ensign."

"Bye, Allison."

Ensign walked back in from the sunny outside weather to pull his clothes from the dryer in the laundromat. He smiled to himself. Ensign had been interacting with Allison on the website since 2018, when he was still living in his house in Perrysburg. She was the only person he knew from the website who lived in Wyoming. Allison had recently moved from Cheyanne to Rock Springs.

Ensign didn't know Allison was there until he made it to Rock Springs on the spare tire. Allison had been out of town on business when Ensign was first in the city. She told him then that she would be happy to see him when she came back. Ensign called her when he returned from Yellowstone.

That evening, Ensign sat in his car amongst the campers and trucks parked in the back section of the Rock Springs Walmart parking lot. He had been working on a project to step up his travel game. Ensign was framing a screen to fit in his passenger window, so he could sleep in his car with a breeze at night and avoid mosquitos and other bugs.

Allison pulled up in her new silver extended-cab pickup truck. She parked next to Ensign and stepped out of her truck. Ensign stood up from his car and walked around the front to interact. They both smiled at each other.

Allison was ex-military. She was a couple of years younger than Ensign. She was only five feet tall. Allison had long, straight, black hair down to her mid-back. Her skin was bronzed and flawless. Her smile warmed his heart. She was as beautiful as Ensign knew she would be.

The two of them talked for an hour at the edge of that Walmart parking lot. They watched the Sun set from their elevated and unobstructed vantage point. They laughed and smiled. Their conversation was interesting. Suddenly, Allison seemed to have something else to say.

"Ok, come on. Follow me in your car. I want to take you somewhere. We'll drop your car off in my driveway. You'll see."

Ensign had no reservations. He walked back around his car to his driver's seat. He was ready for whatever adventure Allison had in mind. Allison got in her truck. Ensign pulled out through the parking lot behind her. Ten minutes later, he parked in her driveway. He hopped up into the passenger side of her truck. Ensign buckled his seatbelt, ready for the ride.

Allison drove to the back of the newly built subdivision at the base of a mountain. She turned from her neighborhood onto the street running along the side of the mountain. She then turned off the road onto a dirt and gravel road; up the side of the mountain.

Ensign recorded video during the off-road adventure. The truck wound its way up the side of the mountain. The truck's headlights were bright enough to show Ensign something. At any moment, if Allison hadn't been sure with her driving, they could plunge off the side to their deaths. Ensign tried to hold the camera steady as the bumps and rocks bounced the truck around while they climbed the steep mountain pass. Ensign saw the lights of Rock Springs in the nighttime distance below them.

They reached the top of the mountain. The summit, along with all else in Wyoming, was windswept and barren. Allison pulled up to park on the dirt and rocks overlooking the valley below. The city below them was lit up in the nighttime. Ensign could see across the valley to where the mountains on the other side of the city met with the starry sky above them. Ensign could feel the pickup truck swaying in the wind.

Allison and Ensign both saw the headlights behind them as a car pulled up. A moment later, two officers walked up to the sides of the truck. The location was a common spot for people to visit to smoke marijuana. Neither Allison nor Ensign smoked pot. The officers ran their driver's licenses back at their cruiser. An officer returned a moment later to hand them back their licenses. The headlights remained behind them for another five minutes...then the police car pulled away to head back down the mountain.

It was hard to open the truck door against the high winds at the top of the barren mountain. Ensign managed to hop out of the truck to survey the area. He recorded video of a strange and otherworldly weather station structure close to where they had parked. Ensign hopped back up into the truck. Allison leaned over to him, and they began to kiss.

A first happened for Ensign that night in the truck atop the mountain with Allison. It wasn't a first he ever wanted. As they undressed each other, Allison told him she wanted him inside her. Allison told him it wasn't possible for her to climax from oral sex. Ensign told her he wished to try anyhow. He had heard that before, and he had proven other women wrong every single time. After half an hour with his mouth between her legs… Ensign conceded to Allison. It was the first time he wasn't able to make good on his oral delivery.

Allison told Ensign how good it had felt. She also told him how she was basically lacking a clitoris. She didn't need to mention that. Ensign knew it within a few moments of when he began licking her. Though he had done drugs earlier that day, Ensign had no issue getting up with her. After the attempt at oral, they consummated together in any positions they could manage in the extended cab of Allison's pickup truck. Fortunately, with intercourse, Ensign managed to get Allison to the point she hadn't reached with oral.

The two of them spent the next few hours watching the stars over the valley. Ensign thanked Allison for sharing such an amazing night with him. He thanked her for showing him such a wonderful location. Ensign held on as he bounced around on the treacherous drive back down the mountain. Allison and Ensign kissed for a few minutes when they arrived again at Allison's house.

Allison had relatives staying with her at the time, so Ensign was unable to stay the night with her. Ensign smiled at Allison. Allison told him to see her again. Ensign told her the truth: it was the only time he had ever been to Wyoming after forty years of life…the probability of a return was rather low. She understood. They kissed again. It was bittersweet. Ensign thought about Allison as he left Rock Springs that night.

Back to Earth

Ensign had a long drive ahead of him. His goal was to reach Cheyanne, on the other side of the state. He got gas in his car at the same rest stop from which he left to journey to Yellowstone a few days prior. He decided to fuel himself as he fueled up his car. Ensign blasted down a series of huge hotrails. He blasted off from that rest stop fully fueled...and fully fueled.

Ensign hit the nighttime highway with determination. The travel lanes, except for the big rigs as expected, were all but empty. Ensign turned up the music and set up his phone in the windshield phone holder to record the trip. He thought back to the speeds he hit on the drive west across Nebraska. He decided that drive had been practice for the drive east across Wyoming. With the music hitting, and the drugs hitting, Ensign hit the gas.

Again, Ensign peaked at one hundred and forty miles per hour. He kept the speed up for much longer lengths of time on his drive to Cheyanne. He ripped past semis as they meandered along at about eighty. He weaved through multiple vehicles on the rare instances he came up on any traffic at all. Like those days skirting the outsides of Detroit on those interstates, he lifted off the Earth. He was in space.

Ensign's mind raced; his reactions were on point. He was ever diligent to anticipate his roadway maneuvers before he put them into action. The red colors of rear lights on cars shot towards him like he was in a video game. He changed lanes to accommodate. He had fractions of seconds to react and find clear ways forward. Headlights on the cars he passed disappeared behind him into the black of night as fast as he could glance into his mirrors.

Time passed; Ensign was too focused to measure how long. Miles passed; he kept a staggering pace. He knew it was the fastest he had ever covered the distance he covered that night. The speed (and the speed) kept his mind in an adrenaline-saturated state. Ensign began seeing road signs for Cheyanne. He made it. As traffic picked up, approaching the city in the middle of the night, Ensign governed his speed, as he stayed on the cusp of the triple-digit mark.

When he reached the city proper, Ensign came back to Earth and obeyed the speed limit. That drive through the desolate expanse of Wyoming in the darkness of night was a metaphor for a portal; one which returned him from an otherworldly and magical land, where nature was the focus. Ensign was back to the daily life of cities, and people, and activity...and stresses, and worries, and concerns, and limits to the visions of what was out there beyond a manufactured world of clutter; where focus only extended to that which was immediately and currently visible.

Ensign stuck around the city for a day. He went back to the park in Cheyanne the next morning to get some sunlight and work more on his car audio. Ensign again ate at a Mexican restaurant. He drove around more and explored the city. The point came when he knew it was time to go. He knew he could lazily work his way down to New Mexico to pick up his tattoo gun when it arrived at the Whole Foods locker, but he had done his time in Wyoming.

Ensign came upon Fort Collins, Colorado in the middle of the night. As always, he was busy sending and replying to messages on all his social media platforms and apps. He had been in contact with a guy who lived in the city. The guy was looking to party. He invited Ensign over.

Though he took steps to remove himself from the drug trade, Ensign still used crystal all day, every day. The guy in Fort Collins mentioned he had his own crystal. That was fine with Ensign. He still had an ounce from the last time he acquired crystal in the Midwest, and he planned to leave it in his car when he reached the guy's house...unless the quality of the guy's drugs was disgraceful, and he needed to go back out and retrieve his own to make the party happen.

The crystal in Fort Collins turned out to be quite acceptable. Ensign never needed to make anyone aware he had his own. Ensign did leave the house earlier that next morning than he anticipated. The surprise of the guy's boyfriend seeking to watch their activity turned him off from the interaction.

A trans girl on the other side of Fort Collins scooped Ensign up online shortly after he was back in his car. Ensign headed over to her place. He parked outside the apartment, where he was told his car wouldn't be towed, and he went inside. There was a strong connection between the two of them. They shared intimacy. They then slept for an hour that early morning before the girl had to leave for work. Ensign left Fort Collins. He continued working his way south from northern Colorado to Santa Fe, New Mexico.

By summer of 2020, Ensign had been on the website for two and a half years. He was on all the popular dating apps for almost as long. Popularity online in an adult hookup world became strategic. As he traveled, he matched with people in close proximity via geolocation on the internet and apps. As he traveled through cities, he would begin interacting with many of his matches. Ensign had many conversations going on at once with those close to where he traveled.

Ensign's conversations revealed which matches wanted him to stop to see them as he was passing through the area. Messages were received letting him know availability and locations. Often, when matches weren't available at the moment...whether they were at work or somehow otherwise occupied, they let Ensign know when they were next available and wished to see him.

Ensign's travel throughout the country had him crisscrossing locations many times over. Along the way, new matches popped up anytime he was back through any area where he had already been. The new conversations with the new matches began as he was still connected to previous matches in the area.

Sometimes, Ensign adjusted his travel to line up with certain matches and their availability. As he drove, he sent messages to his connections; whichever upcoming city he was approaching. Some people were available. Ensign stopped to see them and hung out. Others weren't free at the moment, so they made plans to try again on Ensign's next pass.

Ensign's interactions weren't based only on intimate experiences. Though some of his matches were only seeking no-strings-attached hookups, Ensign was always happy to just see people and go with the flow; whatever ways their time together was spent. The length of time spent was as varied as their activities together.

It was always exciting to create those dynamics with people all around the country. Some instances ended up being one-time things. With other people, sustained dynamics always gave Ensign something he could look forward to when he was passing through a certain location in the country.

Meaningful friendships and long-term intimate dynamics popped up and lasted as he traveled. Unique situations created interesting memories in the times when those one-time meetings didn't blossom into the future. Very rarely, meet-ups went far off the rails. Usually, the worst-case scenario ended with Ensign's knowledge that the connection hadn't lined up, and he wouldn't be making a point to see that person again.

Ensign had more and more connected people and places while he kept up on his travels. No matter where he was, in almost any location in any state in the country, Ensign knew he had places he could go to and people he could see. He felt alive as he traveled. He felt alive creating and sustaining dynamics with people everywhere. Ensign felt secure; knowing he had places close by where he could visit, no matter where he was in the country.

Ensign had friends with whom he could go out to dinner... or just go get ice cream. He'd stop and meet people to hike in a park. He'd stop for sleepovers. He knew who wished to party, and Ensign could stop and get high with someone and talk for an afternoon before he continued on down the road. When he was tired, he'd be invited to come take naps with people and rest. People would show Ensign around their cities, the best locations for stunning nature photography and videos. Others wished to create videos and memories of an adult nature.

By summer of 2020, due to all the interactions and connections Ensign cultivated, he felt comfortable and familiar almost everywhere in the United States. He collected so many wonderful and meaningful memories...shared with people who became important to him on so many levels, in so many different ways. He was appreciative of the love and concern he felt from everywhere.

Ensign's dream had come true; he felt alive...but he hadn't fixed himself. He was happy, but he wasn't. He knew he had created a life of note. He knew he was living each day, not just going through the motions. His time felt full and immediate, and he lived in most moments. Ensign was doing what he wanted, and he felt free...but something was still off.

The One that Counts

Ensign thought back to the dawn of 2018, getting accustomed to online interactions. He remembered newly being invited to houses all around the country. He remembered feeling how suddenly the world had opened up in front of him. He remembered that first spark of an idea to travel and experience life.

Ensign pulled into Dean's driveway in Aurora, Colorado. It was two and a half years after he was first invited to see Dean. Ensign thought back to how foreign the invitation had felt as he sat in his living room in Ohio and interacted with Dean. He thought how so much had happened between that night Dean invited Ensign to see him and that current evening in mid-2020; as he stepped from his car to walk up Dean's driveway.

Dean

Ensign accepted Dean's offer back in the winter of 2018. He told Dean that someday he would make good on his acceptance to visit him. Ensign didn't know when, and he didn't know how...but he told him it would happen.

Dean was one of the fans from the website who had followed him from the very beginning of his plunge into adult hookup culture. They maintained contact and a friendship, through all else which was life, over those couple of years. Dean was a friend Ensign touched base with periodically. Dean's life went on entirely independently from his own until Ensign knocked on the front door of Dean's house in mid-2020.

Ensign's life, since 2018, had seemed surreal in many ways.

Whenever he told someone that he would visit them, and then when he made good on his promise, so much happened in the time between. The surrealistic feeling as Ensign was in the moment of meeting someone always had him beside himself.

Ensign remembered those earlier moments when he accepted invitations to visit...and he couldn't believe it had somehow suddenly become that moment when he was making good on his word. Time, events, locations...all which happened and did not happen between the invite and the actual visit; it was a journey in its own way to get from that point A to point B. Invite...all everything in life...visit; it had Ensign shaking his head.

Ensign stayed the night at Dean's house, but he left after breakfast early in the morning. Ensign told Dean he would see him again on his return from New Mexico. The pink and red sky of the sunrise over Aurora, Colorado that morning was beautiful. Ensign recorded video after he filled up his car's gas tank. Ensign then headed south, away from the Denver metro area.

The mountains out Ensign's passenger side windows were constant as he drove south on I-25. He was driving parallel to the eastern edge of the Rocky Mountains. The snow-peaked caps of the tallest mountains loomed high above. The wall of natural beauty extended as far north and south as the eye could see. Some of those largest mountains were fourteeners. Colorado has more peaks above fourteen thousand feet than any other state.

As he came up to Colorado Springs, the wall of mountains to Ensign's west crept ever closer to the highway. As he passed through the city, some mountains on the eastern ridge of the Rockies were on both sides of the road. Colorado Springs was split by the highway. Ensign got off I-25 at an exit on the west side of the road. He followed the exit up and around the curves, onto the elevated surface streets of Colorado Springs.

Ensign's view from the eastern side of the city consumed his thoughts. He sought a vantage point to overlook the highway below, out to the wall of mountains beyond. There was a parking lot outside a strip of shops in the right location. Ensign pulled in, and he parked facing out over the highway below.

It was a great spot with a spectacular western-facing view of the Rocky Mountains. It was the perfect spot to spend a couple hours doing drugs, enjoying the scenery, and interacting online. After an hour of hotrails, Ensign reached a point in a conversation where he knew his perfect location wasn't perfect for what was about to transpire. He knew he needed to find somewhere slightly further up the mountain, in a more secluded area.

Ensign packed up his drug paraphernalia and pulled out of the parking lot. He took the winding road higher up onto the mountain; away from the traffic and people in the busier and more populus section of Colorado Springs. Ensign found another parking lot which suited his needs.

With the shades up in his car windows, Ensign videoed with a friend of his until she climaxed. It was far too hot in Ensign's car for him to finish. He tried. He felt he was close two times during the interaction. Each time he felt close, the heat overtook him. After she finished, Ensign let his friend know he wasn't going to be able to climax for her. Their video call ended.

After he put his pants back on, Ensign took the window shades down and rolled down all his windows. The breeze, high up on the mountainside, was as much of an instant relief to him that Ensign may as well have climaxed with the wind flowing through his car and around him. He was pouring sweat. Ensign dried himself with a towel, and the sweat kept coming as he began to cool down.

Ensign picked up his phone after he put on a shirt. He wanted to check the map. When the map came up, he saw something interesting. He'd heard of Pike's Peak, despite having never been in close proximity. Ensign wasn't even sure why he knew things about the mountain. He learned something else as he looked at the map while he sat in his car on a mountainside in Colorado Springs; he learned he was within a half-hour's drive to the base of Pike's Peak.

There were storm clouds around some random spots in the mountains in both directions to the horizon. From what Ensign could see, most of the peaks were sunny. He tried to figure out which peak was Pike's Peak. His vantage point was particularly good. Ensign managed to sort out the many mountains in his frame of vision from the opposite side of I-25. The mountain which he determined to be Pike's Peak, towering into the sky beyond shorter peaks, was clearly visible in the sunshine. A wave of excitement hit him with the breeze coming through his car windows. He had his plans for the day.

Ensign drove down from the mountainside on the eastern side of I-25. He drove through the commotion of mid-morning Colorado Springs to the west. Within five minutes, the world around him shifted completely. Ensign had just been in the center of Colorado Springs; surrounded by buildings, pavement, people, and cars. He had just been waiting at stoplights while people walked and drove all around him. He had just been in a heavily populated and trafficked urban location; surrounded by businesses and residences. All it took was five minutes of driving for his entire world to become something else entirely.

When Ensign reached the point where the city abruptly stopped, nature took over with an impressive and astounding switch of environment; pine trees and forests, giant red rocks and roadside drop-offs alluded to the base of a wild mountainous region. Flowing cascading water, cliffs as high up as he could see. Sharp curves on steep inclines kept him at full attention. Ensign was suddenly in the Rocky Mountain wilderness. The complete shift all around him came fast. His brain was still adjusting when he realized he was quickly ascending in elevation.

Ensign had to give more gas to his car's engine. He was angled back as he climbed upward into the mountains. He didn't have a full tank of gas, but he figured he had enough to summit Pike's Peak. By the time he reached the entranceway gate of the mountain, Ensign had already ascended well above the city below him. He could no longer see any reminder of civilization besides the road and the traffic also heading to the top of the mountain.

There was a parking area at the gate to the summit of Pike's Peak. Shuttle busses were loading up passengers and dropping others off in the parking lot. Ensign drove past the loading area. He paid money at the gate to drive himself to the top. Ensign started to record video from out of his front windshield as the gate in front of him lifted to allow his car through. He read the signs on the side of the road to the summit, and he mentally prepared his drug-filled brain for the drive.

Ensign passed a lake early on in the drive. Then he crossed a bridge. There was forest all around him. He kept climbing higher. As time passed, his shoulders began to ache from the constant motion of the steering wheel. His ankle began to cramp from the constant adjustment of the gas pedal. Periodically, especially around corners, the view out above the mountains was visible. Ensign kept climbing higher in his car.

A while later, Ensign saw a stop-point in the road ahead. It was a checkpoint. He pulled up to one of the workers standing on the side of the lane. The worker explained that, for him to continue ascending the mountain, it was mandatory that they check his car's brakes. The worker explained what was coming up on the drive.

Though the distance remaining to drive to reach the summit of Pike's Peak was only a small fraction of the distance he had just driven, Ensign was warned it was going to take him a longer amount of time. The road was about to become much steeper, and Ensign was about to encounter many more turns; turns which were much sharper and more dangerous. Ensign's brakes passed the test, and he left the checkpoint.

Ensign drove straight forward from the checkpoint. The trees lining both sides of the road were thick. He couldn't see anything beyond them. The road curved again; up and around...and suddenly Ensign was above the tree line. Not only could Ensign see the view around him, but he also saw to the ends of the world. He could see the deeper blue in the atmosphere above the curvature of the horizon. Beyond the endless sea of mountains, Ensign saw above everything which was of the world. Ensign saw where Heaven came down and met with Earth. He smiled. His choice to summit Pike's Peak was the correct choice.

Once he crossed over to that strange world above the tree line, Ensign felt he was in an alien environment. The ground towards the top of the mountain was otherworldly; tan rocks of all sizes; the entire environment up above the trees and clouds. The top section of Pike's Peak was barren and uniform...and it was amazing.

The road, as Ensign was warned, became immediately and drastically more treacherous. His car struggled at the angle of incline. The curves bent back completely towards the opposite directions from which Ensign approached them. He could see the winding road crisscrossing directly above him. He drove straight for a stretch, then he curved up and around. He was then driving another straight stretch, but in the opposite direction.

The curves had to be taken blind around some of the rock structures on the side of the mountain. Some locations, where possible, had small sections of guard rails. Mostly though, the road wasn't wide enough for guard rails; the ascending lane and descending lane were in a space just big enough for only the two lanes. The sheer drop-offs where the pavement of the lane ended was open air to thousands of feet below. Ensign loved it; his Lexus did not.

Earlier on the drive, Ensign passed through a layer of clouds. The sky was clear when he reached the final curve to the parking location at the summit of Pike's Peak. A parking attendant directed the line of cars to different open spaces in the parking rows. Ensign was amazed at how many cars were parked in the rocks and gravel at the top of the mountain. He found a spot, four rows into the lot, and he parked.

Ensign's car had been smoking from under the hood since he

reached the parking attendant. Ensign turned off his car and popped the hood. When he opened the hood, it created a plume of smoke, the only cloud at the summit of Pike's Peak. The coolant in the tank was boiling. Ensign knew the engine was far too hot to attempt to find what was wrong.

Ensign closed the hood and got back in his car. It was cold at the top of the mountain, and it was windy. He pulled out a jacket from one of his bags. Ensign opened another bag. He set up the tray and poured a line of crystal onto it.

Ensign heated the end of a glass stem with his propane torch. He put the cool end of the pipe into his nostril. He plugged his other nostril with his fingers against the side of his nose. In a sweeping motion, his head went down across the tray. The hot end of the pipe, barely above the line of crystal, vaporized the crystal as Ensign sucked it up into his nose. He then blew out the largest cloud at the summit of the mountain...except the cloud which was still escaping from under his hood.

The drugs hit fast. The feeling overshadowed Ensign's worry about his mechanical issues. He decided, as he zipped up his drug equipment and placed the bag under his seat, he wasn't going to let his car problems dampen an experience he knew was about to be amazing. Ensign got out of his car and put on his jacket. He knew he was going to create memories from a life experience...on the summit of Pike's Peak.

Ensign left his car to cool off, and he began to hike up the rock incline to reach the peak of the mountain. The air was thin, and Ensign was out of breath constantly. Every few steps, he had to stop to catch his breath. He was breathing heavily as he walked up towards the summit. Ensign made it up and around the final rock formation, and suddenly he was standing on the summit of Pike's Peak...trying to catch his breath.

People were wandering around up on the rocks. Some were standing still, taking in the amazing three-hundred-and-sixty-degree view of infinity. Others were taking pictures and video. Ensign began taking pictures and video as well. It was amazing to be able to stand at the top of the world and look out over all of creation. Ensign appreciated every minute he spent up there. He knew the drive down the mountain would be beautiful, and treacherous, and hard on his brakes...if his car even started again when he went to leave. He didn't care. He was, again, in a timeless moment. It all made sense.

...

The concern for Ensign's car was with him as he drove south through Colorado. He stopped at rest stops frequently. He continued checking his car, but the overheating issue seemed to have cooled off. Weeks prior, Ensign left Lansing without his exhaust system and catalytic converters being replaced. Ensign had been putting many hard miles on his car. That thought stayed with him as he drove closer to his destination in New Mexico. The drugs kept him going as he drove through the night.

Plugging Along

Back when Ensign was twenty-one years old, he lived with four friends in Toledo, Ohio. The rave and party-drug scene were big in their lives. Ketamine was a staple at their house. Though they all partied all the time, one particular friend/roommate and Ensign really loved ketamine. The two of them did ketamine far more often, and in larger quantities, than their other friends; much more than everyone else who partied at their house.

Ketamine is a dissociative with unique properties. The goal was to always do enough of the drug to be put in a state known as a "k-hole." In a k-hole, the outside world ceased to exist. The experience became a journey through the mind. The experience, like a dream, lacked the boundaries and reality of the physical world.

Ensign fell into a recurrent k-hole. The experience was based in what Ensign perceived to be the center of the Earth. Stone pillars stood in formation in a round area. Their heights increased, as would the seats in an amphitheater, as they moved out from the center. In the very center, a glowing fire; the pillars centered around the fire. The light in the center of the Earth was red. Everything was tinted red.

In his k-holes, Ensign floated in an egg-shaped pod as he orbited the center fire of the Earth. In countless similar pods also orbiting the fire, there were others. Though Ensign didn't interact with the other pods, nor did their existence affect him in any way, he could vaguely sense the pods were occupied with co-workers and others from his real life.

In his k-holes, Ensign's orbit speed increased as he flowed

around the fire in the center of the Earth. If he remained in the k-hole, his orbit would spiral outward, away from the fire. As he picked up speed, he felt the physicality of his being slip away. The faster Ensign spiraled outward, the freer and more unattached to the physical world he felt. Ensign's orbit left inner Earth and entered outer space. The faster he went, the wider his orbit, the farther outward into the universe Ensign flew.

During one particular k-hole, Ensign reached the highest orbit speed, as far out into space as he had ever been. His connection with his physical body and the physical world slipped away. He felt everything fall away behind him. Ensign felt himself leaving his body, a mere vessel, as he became one with the universe beyond him. Ensign felt his physical form no longer incumbering him as he became energy hurdling through space. Ensign's cares and worries of life left him. He became one with everything as he dissipated into nothing...as he became all the universe around him. Ensign felt the last tiny twinge of all he was as a person as it fell away...and he let go...and he was free... then he woke up.

Ensign was almost to New Mexico. The sky was clear as dawn broke. The sunrise over Trinidad, Colorado was exceptionally beautiful as the light in the sky illuminated the squared-off peak of Trinidad's landmark natural monolith. Perched high above the highway at a rest stop halfway up a mountain's side to the west of the interstate, Ensign gazed to the east as the Sun illuminated Simpson's Rest. He was twenty-one miles from the New Mexico border, but Ensign was two days shy of his delivery arriving in Santa Fe.

Ensign sat, deep in thought, and he surveyed across the valley to the rock formation on the other side of the interstate. His view that morning was breathtaking. Had he not been there to see it, he wondered if it all would have still been there; existing without him. The crystal had been working on Ensign's brain as he drove through Colorado into that morning. He wondered; was that sunrise real...or was it all just an illusion? Could it have been that all Ensign thought was real was only real to him? When he took that long ride, would all else cease to exist?

Ensign snapped out of it. He was tired, and his brain had been running on fumes through the night. From his vantage point, the city of Trinidad looked interesting. Ensign decided to explore the area for the day...beginning with the top of Simpson's Rest. Down the mountain, across the interstate, through the city, and up the other mountain; he had his path. Ensign started his car.

Two online interactions were significant to Ensign while he spent the day in Trinidad. A guy named Justin in some small city in northern New Mexico; Justin convinced Ensign to stop and see him on his way to Santa Fe. A woman named Stacey in Pueblo, Colorado; Ensign agreed to stop and see Stacey on his northern trip from New Mexico when he returned later in the week.

Ensign walked around underneath a viaduct in downtown Trinidad and recorded video of a storm as it moved in to shroud Simpson's Rest in rain. Ensign texted Justin to let him know he would see him around midday the next day. Ensign waited until the thunderstorm swept through the area late that afternoon before he decided to get back in his car and drive south. As the Sun went down that evening, Ensign crossed into New Mexico on the interstate.

Ensign again felt that twinge of excitement as he approached the border of a state he had never before been. It never failed... even if Ensign had done so much crystal that he couldn't get any higher from drugs, the thrill of exploring the unknown still registered on his chemically fried brain. New Mexico was the forty-eighth state on his list which he was finally able to check off. He felt satisfied with his plan to drive to Santa Fe to pick up his new tattoo machine.

The feeling wore off quickly. It was pitch black as Ensign drove through the mountain pass at the border of Colorado and New Mexico. The sky cast an eerie vibe that night. There was something ominous about. Ensign didn't know why he felt a foreboding uneasiness. The drugs, after being awake for many hours, were beyond the point of keeping him going.

Ensign found a rest stop in the emptiness and black of night. He felt alone; beyond just actually being alone. He felt on edge. All the vehicles at the rest stop were semitrucks. Ensign didn't see a single person outside, or in the restrooms. After he got back to his car from the bathroom, Ensign put the shades up in his windows. He took his handgun from his ankle holster and placed it in his lap. With his gun in his lap, Ensign immediately passed out from sleep deprivation.

Ensign woke up the next morning in the Wild West. Sleep, as it always had, cured his previously onsetting paranoia. The dread and fear of the prior night had dissipated with the darkness. It was bright and sunny outside. Ensign's sense of wonder filled him with the desire to keep on course. The hotrails which filled his lungs as he was parked there in the New Mexico scenery reinvigorated his well-rested mind. Ensign's resolve to reach Santa Fe filled him with excitement.

Justin had been sending text messages while Ensign was asleep. Ensign replied to him. Justin gave Ensign an address, and he asked what time Ensign was going to be over to his house to see him. After Ensign put the address into his phone's map, he told Justin he would see him at two o'clock. By four o'clock, Ensign was back on the road and headed south, away from Justin's house and closer to Santa Fe.

Borrowed Time

Ensign booked the suite for three nights. The third-floor balcony of Ensign's hotel room overlooked a large courtyard. Ensign walked inside and set down his bags in the first room of his suite. He walked through the kitchen and through another room. Ensign then reached his bedroom. The view from that side of Ensign's suite overlooked a parking lot, out into the city of Santa Fe. He was happy with the lodging.

As he waited for his visitor that first evening, Ensign showered. Drugs were laid out on one of the desks in the bedroom. Earlier that afternoon, Ensign picked up his order from the locker at the grocery store a few miles away. Ensign's new tattoo machine was set up on another desk, over by the bedroom window.

Ensign had three packages waiting for him in the locker: his new rotary tattoo machine, another amplifier for his car stereo, and spark plugs. The rotary tattoo machine was rated as the best machine of 2020. The amplifier was going to be the fifth in the system Ensign was perpetually building in his car; used exclusively to power two ten-inch subwoofers which he previously installed to complement the two twelve-inch subwoofers in his trunk. The spark plugs, items in Ensign's car which he knew needed to be changed out, were going to be put in once he was back in Colorado later in the week.

Ensign's phone had multiple new text messages. He saw them once he finished showering. A couple of the texts were from Justin. Ensign ignored them. That stop, earlier in the day, was awkward and odd. Justin gave off a desperate and clingy vibe the whole time Ensign was at his house.

Justin was twenty-four years old and closeted. He constantly talked about how he had an important job working for the court system of his small city. Justin spent much of the interaction trying to convince Ensign to stay with him long-term. It was the first time Ensign met Justin, having only first interacted with him while in Trinidad the day prior. Justin's messages to Ensign after Ensign left for Santa Fe were focused on how Ensign needed to come back and stay with him.

Though he didn't blatantly tell Justin in text response to leave him alone, Ensign absolutely ignored his pestering. Ensign set those particular text messages from Justin to silent on his phone after his shower. Ensign switched his focus to another text conversation. As he dried off, he responded to a beautiful twenty-year-old trans girl. They had begun texting as Ensign arrived in Santa Fe. She was on her way to Ensign's hotel.

"I'll be to your hotel in a half hour."

"Sounds good. I'm out of the shower. I'll meet you in the front parking lot when you get here. This hotel is big and confusing. It'll be easier if I just come out to walk you in."

"Ok, I'll text when I arrive...I'm hungry."

"We'll order food when you get here. See you soon."

Ensign walked the girl back out to her car late that night. He made his way back through the corridors and courtyards to his suite. Ensign was excited to use his new tattoo machine for the first time. He had another assignment from Shannon. Ensign had been directed to tattoo a blue lightning bolt on his left ball to compliment the green lightning bolt Shannon previously required he tattoo on his right ball.

As with the green lightning bolt, the blue bolt bled a decent amount. The new tattoo machine worked very well, but the particular location of the tattoo again proved to be a challenge. Ensign did drugs through the night as he interacted with

Shannon; giving her updates on progress as he continued to fill in the spots where blood kept the ink from remaining under his skin.

Overall, it took six separate applications during that stay in the suite in New Mexico to complete the tattoo. Ensign spent the three days exploring Santa Fe, tattooing himself, and intimately interacting with Shannon as he progressed. One of the other interactions during that time was with Stacey, the woman in Pueblo, Colorado.

Stacey was a forty-year-old blonde woman from the website. Stacey and Ensign shared exceptionally good conversation in those few days. They made plans. Once Ensign left New Mexico, he planned a stop in Pueblo, Colorado on his return trip North. They planned to spend the weekend together, since Stacey's teenage children were at their dad's house that weekend. Stacey also had a place for Ensign to work on his car; he could install the new amplifier and change the spark plugs.

Ninety Seconds to Midnight

The nature of the dream startled him awake. He looked over. Stacey was still asleep. Ensign walked to the bathroom as he tried to shake off the remnants of the nightmare. He put his tray down on the bathroom counter and looked into the mirror to be sure his previous night's haircut was evenly lined up. Ensign was satisfied. He broke up a line of crystal and heated his glass stem with a new torch Stacey had given him when he arrived the night before. Stacey smoked pot, but she had no need for the torch; she didn't do crystal. As he blew out a large plume of smoke, the last of Ensign's post-nightmare feelings went into the air with the cloud.

The task at hand proved more difficult and time-consuming than Ensign anticipated. It was hot outside, high nineties. He was pouring sweat and exhausted by the time he managed to change his car's spark plugs. Ensign had been out in the direct sunlight for a few hours. A couple of the spark plugs took extreme effort and odd ingenuity to break free of their position. Ensign banged up his hands, and he was covered in grease from the engine. It was mid-afternoon when he finally finished and walked back into Stacey's house.

Two days before that, Ensign had been driving around exploring the natural scenery in Santa Fe. As he drove up a winding mountain road in a national park just outside the city, Ensign's car again overheated as it had during his summit of Pike's Peak. He ended up stranded on an overlook in the wilderness of the park. Ensign spent three hours in the forest, on the side of a mountain, while he tried to sort out what was going on under the hood.

Ensign plugged his code reader into the computer of his Lexus. He scanned his car. The Bluetooth results appeared on his phone screen: Ensign's Lexus had forty-nine separate error codes on the code reader.

After adjustments to different components of the engine, and after waiting for his car to cool off, Ensign was able to drive back down the mountain to civilization. That nagging feeling of the impending doom to his car was amplified and pushed to the forefront of his thoughts. Again, his car had stopped working upon ascension of a steep mountain. Again, his coolant reservoir held boiling coolant. Again, he drove away knowing it was only a matter of time until the problems wouldn't allow him to drive farther.

After he left Stacey's house, Ensign reached Denver with no discernable car trouble. The pressure in his mind eased back. Ensign put his bags down on the second bed of his hotel room. Ensign was close to the Denver airport. His new spark plugs held up on the recent drive north from Stacey's house in Pueblo.

Ensign checked his phone. He read the most recent message. Ensign replied back to the woman from the website.

"I made it to Denver. I'm in my room."

"Ok, I'm leaving my brother's house now. I'll be over in forty-five minutes."

After two hours with the woman in his hotel room, she dressed; ready to leave.

"Well, I'm satisfied for sure. Thanks for being my first White guy. Your mouth is amazing. I'm happy I came over to meet you."

"I enjoyed it as well. I'll walk you to your car."

When Ensign got back from the parking lot, he covered the smoke detector in his room with a plastic grocery bag. Ensign set up his drug paraphernalia and his tattoo equipment. He picked up his phone and began scrolling the messages he missed during the previous two hours.

Bobby met Ensign close to the hotel at a favorite sandwich shop chain restaurant; one which Ensign was happy to see existed out West. Bobby was dropped off as Ensign was sitting in his car eating his sandwich. Ensign offered him one of the quarters of the roast beef on sourdough. Bobby took a bite, and he told Ensign he saw why Ensign liked the restaurant so much. They sat and ate. Once finished, Ensign drove them back to his hotel.

Ensign began interacting with Bobby on an app after the woman from the website left that afternoon. Bobby was twenty-eight years old. He was a White guy, originally from Michigan. Through his military service, he had been in Denver, Colorado for the better part of a decade. Trouble after his discharge kept Bobby out in Denver on probation, after a short stint in prison.

Bobby and Ensign got along like lifelong friends. Bobby couldn't do crystal with Ensign on account of random drug testing, but he had no issue with Ensign's indulgence. Bobby drank alcohol instead, of which Ensign had no interest. The two days with Bobby familiarized Ensign with the city of Denver.

Bobby and Ensign went all over the place; friends' houses to party, hotels to meet others, restaurants, bars, and shopping centers. Ensign saw all sides of Denver proper. Downtown, suburbs, inner city, business districts...it was a lot of exploration in such a brief time. Ensign's car was still holding up, but he worried about it. He felt he was pushing his limits.

After those two days, Bobby and Ensign parted ways. Ensign dropped Bobby off at a duplex where two of his friends lived. Bobby invited Ensign in to hang out for a bit before Ensign took off to leave Colorado. Ensign had a weird feeling in that moment, and he opted to decline. He didn't wish to meet Bobby's friends. He didn't wish to hang out in a house. He wished to get on the road and head away from Colorado.

As Bobby walked up to his friends' house, Ensign pulled out of the neighborhood. The southern area of Denver was extremely traffic congested. Ensign managed to find a gas station five minutes down the road. He pulled in and parked. He was amazed how many cars were filling the roads and parking lots. People were everywhere as well, walking all around him.

Ensign's paranoia got the best of him. While parked at that gas station, Ensign stepped from his car and checked for any signs of tracking devices. Ensign hopped back in his car, blew down some more hotrails, and pulled up map directions from the heart of Denver towards Wyoming.

Ensign had one more state in the continental United States to check off his list. Though he knew he wouldn't be able to check off Alaska, he could at least get that forty-ninth state checked off; Oregon. A woman from the website; one whom Ensign had been involved with for the prior year; she lived in Washington. She wanted Ensign to come be with her. Ensign planned to travel a route which took him through Oregon to reach her in Tacoma, Washington.

Ensign reached an interstate highway south of downtown Denver. He began driving north through the metro area. His car seemed like it was running rough. By the time Ensign cleared downtown Denver; on his way to the northern outskirts of the city, the air in his car had become hazy.

The Sun was going down for the night, and the air around the city also seemed hazy. Ensign didn't think much of it, but his worry for the car began to build as the engine began to run rougher. On the highway north of Denver, Ensign's worry was confirmed when smoke began to fill the car from his air vents.

Ensign knew instantly; he was in trouble. He tried to look for exit signs and places within range to drive. Traffic was still filling the interstate as he drove north in desperation to find an exit from the highway. Then, as he was driving in the middle of the interstate, at seventy miles per hour, in the midst of heavy traffic...Ensign's car shut off. The engine, the lights, the music, the power steering...instantly gone. Ensign was surrounded by vehicles on an interstate highway; all traveling at high rates of speed. That last bit of sunlight disappeared in the sky as Ensign's car filled with smoke...and he was suddenly overwhelmed with dread.

Block Universe

In his early thirties, around the time he began dating his second wife, Ensign ran a North American dispatch operation for a fleet of trucks. The car parts they transported originated in Mexico. The trucks which shipped the parts came across the border to the United States in Texas and Arizona. Once the semis crossed the border, a countdown began.

Some trucks delivered directly to auto plants in various states. Some delivered to particular company hubs in Ensign's company's network, to be unloaded and reloaded for over-the-road deliveries around the country. Other trucks delivered directly to Ensign's hub/distribution center in Toledo, Ohio. Still other deliveries stopped at Ensign's hub for paperwork and proceeded on to the auto factories in Canada.

Whether it be those long-haul driving teams or the local relay drivers who crossed into Canada, it was Ensign's responsibility to get the car parts to the designated Canadian auto factories in particular time windows; not too early, but definitely not late. Balancing the driver teams and local or regional truck drivers was possible in a perfect world. There is no perfect world.

Truck drivers are required to follow stringent laws related to time allowed driving versus time at rest. Trucks break down, tires blow out. Drivers have personal issues affecting their attendance. Loads miss their pickups. Drivers miss their connecting relay points. Weather, traffic, service hours, fueling, construction and road closures, shortage of personnel, shortage of equipment, delays at stops for pickups and/or delivery, vehicle inspections...those are just some of the many unforeseen but inevitable complications which require adjustment and correction in a timely and effective manner.

One factor on those loads going into Canada gave Ensign more stress than anything else: clearing the trucks at the Canada border for entry. Ensign could explain away almost any other situation which resulted in a truckload of parts not making it to an auto plant in the scheduled time window. Trucks being detained or sent back at the Canada border was a problem with only Ensign held accountable. That issue meant the paperwork Ensign faxed and/or the information he would input into the border patrol's online website had at least one error.

The error could have been as simple as a number being left off of a barcode...or maybe a name was signed on the wrong line. Maybe a sticker was placed on the wrong page of the faxed papers. Maybe the truck identification number hadn't been updated from the previous load assigned to the truck. It could have been, and was, anything...and it turned a simple morning into a nightmare.

Ensign's desk phone, on those days, would begin to ring off the hook at five minutes past six o'clock in the morning. If his phone rang at that specific moment...Ensign knew he was about to be swept up into a whirlwind of stress for the remainder of the day.

The plant managers arrived at their factories at six o'clock each morning. As they walked into their plants towards their offices for their workdays, they noticed that Ensign's trucks were missing from their unloading docks. The five minutes gave them time to get situated. At five minutes after six o'clock, they would make their first phone calls of the day...to Ensign.

Ensign hated those phone calls so much. When it happened, it always began with the same statement.

"This line shutdown is costing ten thousand dollars each minute your truck isn't here, and we don't have the required parts to operate our assembly line...

...

It was dark outside. The Sun had completed its work for the day. It was also hot. Ensign was pouring sweat. When trucks blew by him, Ensign felt himself vibrate from the close proximity of their passing. The haze around him made it even harder to see in the night sky. Ensign sprayed himself with bug repellant, but some mosquitos were not deterred.

The fire was out as of three hours prior. Ensign made no progress attempting to diagnose the issue, let alone fix it. His hands were cut and bleeding. His arms; covered in grease and oil. Ensign sat back down as traffic zipped by him at seventy miles an hour, barely more than a foot to his left. All he could do at that point was wait.

Ensign's car, after leaving Lansing, truly was his home. He had broken free from a way he chose to no longer live. He left the drug market behind, and opted to only possess a large supply of crystal for personal use as he experienced an unfamiliar life. Ensign turned his back on seemingly endless money for peace of mind and reduced stress. None of that mattered in that moment on the side of the highway just north of Denver, Colorado. Ensign had immediate problems consuming his mind, his sole focus.

Ensign's friend Lex, his friend who helped him buy the Lexus in the first place, bought Ensign a Triple A membership as he sat there on the shoulder of that busy interstate. It had been three hours since he somehow managed to maneuver his completely non-functioning car across two lanes of traffic to a stop on the narrow shoulder of the highway.

This time, in his Lexus on the northbound shoulder of Interstate 25, Ensign knew it wasn't that simple. He wasn't renting a room at his friend Jane's house anymore. He was on the other side of the country, in unfamiliar territory. That time, in his Lexus which was his home...Ensign knew he was in trouble.

Whether he liked it or not...Ensign unexpectedly became a resident of Colorado. He managed a couple of hours of sleep in the bed in his hotel room. Ensign walked out, unclothed, onto the balcony of his hotel room. He gazed across the parking lot. Ensign's Lexus was in a parking space in the back row of the parking lot. It was towed there the night before. As he had done during previous car incidents, Ensign rode with the tow truck driver in the cab of his truck. Ensign walked back into his room from the balcony and set up his hotrail supplies.

Ensign woke up. He was on a big purple couch in a big basement of a big house. There were paintings on the walls and sculptures on pedestals. His belongings, all of his travel bags, were on the floor next to the big purple couch. Ensign took a deep breath, and he stood up.

When he stepped upstairs and walked into the kitchen, Ensign squinted from the bright sunlight filling the house, shining in from the many large windows. A place was set for him at the kitchen table. The food smelled wonderful. Ensign took a glass of orange juice and sat down. Ensign smiled at the other two people; already seated at the table. He greeted them, and he began to eat.

"Ensign, would you like seconds?"

"No thank you. I have a lot of work to do. I need to get started."

As Ensign walked back down the stairs, he noted the ornate and intricate woodwork of the railing. He sat down on the big purple basement couch; on one of the sections which wrapped around at an angle from the main section. Ensign pulled out his phone and began watching instructional videos.

It was the third day Ensign had slept there. It was the day when scheduled packages were set to begin arriving at the house. Ensign had a good idea of what he was going to do from studying videos on his phone. As Ensign watched more videos, Unique sent him a text message.

...

Ensign spent most of the previous night out with Unique. The two of them first met on an app three days prior, while Ensign was in the hotel room. Unique was a pretty Black girl. She was twenty-six years old. She lived in Denver.

A day after Ensign left the hotel, he met Unique in person. Ensign was wandering the streets of Aurora; feeling lost and defeated. After a couple of miles of walking in the night, his legs finally needed a break. As he sat with his backpack and a travel bag outside of a busy gas station in inner city Aurora, Unique pulled into the parking lot and picked him up.

It was midnight as they rode through the busy streets of Aurora. Suddenly, out of nowhere, Unique yelled something. She whipped the steering wheel around and made a sharp U-turn across four lanes of traffic.

"That guy's on flakka!"

As the tires screeched from the quick change of direction, Ensign started to ask her what she was doing. He stopped mid-sentence. The words clicked in his head when Ensign saw the person who captured Unique's attention. Ensign's mouth dropped open slightly as he tried to comprehend what he was seeing. Unique pulled into another gas station and parked her car. They sat in the car and watched the guy outside from across the parking lot. He couldn't help himself; Ensign began to record video.

The guy, a White guy, was most likely in his early twenties. He was dressed like a college student. He was decently groomed, had a normal haircut, khaki shorts, tennis shoes, button-up t-shirt, and no unusual physical features. Had the guy been just standing still; he would have been unassuming; blended into the normal menagerie of people out in Aurora that night. His actions, however, were those of people Ensign had seen in videos online. In fact, Ensign felt as if he was watching one of those "dangers of drugs" videos, taking place directly in front of him.

They watched as the flakka guy talked to himself; fully animated hand gestures and head movements accompanied his words. Suddenly he would freeze, no talking or movement, and he stared into nothing. Then, he'd bolt across the parking lot to another side. At one point, flakka guy did a decent imitation of "the robot" dance move; rigidly moving his arms and neck in fast stiff motions.

"I told you! Flakka!"

"This dude needs help…"

"Welcome to Colorado."

"I don't want this guy to get hit by a car, but I also don't want him to wake up in a jail cell. I have no idea how to help him."

Flakka guy suddenly froze again, and then he bolted to the front of the gas station by the entrance. There was a display of gallon containers of windshield washing fluid for sale outside the entrance to the gas station. The flakka guy took a full three minutes to dramatically explain something to the washer fluid display. He then began walking, in slow-motion, towards a guy pumping gas.

"I don't want to get involved, but if he starts fighting that guy at the gas pump, I'm going to have to try to break it up."

Flakka guy, as soon as he reached the guy at the gas pump, turned around and ran off across the road, into the night.

"That was super weird…"

"Alright, I'm pulling out of here."

Unique pulled out from the gas station, back to the road. They came to a stop behind a line of cars at a red light. The light turned green. Suddenly, flakka guy came out of nowhere and zipped in front of the four lanes of moving traffic. He managed to dodge all the cars, and he again ran off into the night…

…

Ensign read Unique's text message as he sat on the big purple couch. Unique told him she would be over in an hour. Ensign told her he would see her then. Out of respect for his current situation, Ensign held off on doing any crystal on the big purple couch in the basement. He chose to wait until he was with Unique as they drove around taking care of the errands; tasks which Ensign needed to accomplish to forward his progress. Unique smoked crystal. She made a water pipe which she used for smoking crystal. The quality of Unique's crystal was, surprisingly, on par with the quality of Ensign's crystal.

Two packages delivered before Unique arrived to pick up Ensign: a sensor and a water pump. Two more showed up while he was out with Unique getting high and buying other needed items: a PCV valve and another sensor. Ensign was still waiting on a particular gauged socket. The socket was scheduled to arrive the following day. The remainder of the needed parts were picked up from local retailers around the Denver area.

The Pygmalion Effect

Ensign's new car club membership provided a limited number of service calls annually. Ensign called Dean, and he asked Dean for a favor. Ensign used another membership service call to have his car towed again. That second tow was from the hotel to the street alongside Dean's house in Aurora, Colorado.

Dean lived with his semi-elderly mother in an immaculate house in one of the more upscale neighborhoods in Aurora. The six-thousand square foot home was a work of art. The previous homeowner had been a master Russian woodworker. Every detail of every part of the home's interior was beautifully crafted: the railing, the floors, the walls, and the furniture. The paintings and sculptures accented the living space. Even the front and backyard were decorated with sculptures and artwork.

Dean owned a hair salon. In 2020, he was out of work due to the coronavirus pandemic. Dean was concerned for his mother's health at the time, but he permitted Ensign to stay in his basement for those first two weeks while Ensign rebuilt his car's engine.

The engine parts had been arriving, Ensign had been watching instructional videos, and the socket he needed to remove the belts from the engine had arrived. Ensign began taking apart his car's engine on the street in Dean's neighborhood. It was a beautiful and sunny Colorado summer morning.

That evening, Ensign finalized plans with a blonde trans girl; one whom he first met when he arrived in Denver earlier in the month, before he went down to New Mexico. Bethany was twenty-five years old. She lived in Denver with roommates, but she rented a penthouse suite in a luxury hotel that evening. Ensign ordered a car from a ride service, and he told Bethany he would be at her hotel in half an hour.

Bethany was beautiful; her vibe was sultry and erotic. Bethany earned her income as an escort. She took the night off work to spend the evening with Ensign. Their time together was off the clock. Bethany told Ensign she felt something between them during their online interactions. Bethany didn't want money to have any bearing on their experience together. If money had been a factor, Ensign wouldn't have made plans to meet her.

Bethany didn't like crystal, so Ensign did hotrails by himself on a table in the dining area of the hotel suite. Bethany preferred another drug. She smoked black tar heroin. Ensign hadn't done heroin since that Thanksgiving night in 2018; where his friend Makayla babysat him to be sure his accidental overdose didn't become a fatality.

The Denver skyline was visible from the top-floor hotel balcony. Ensign did crystal all through the night. Bethany and Ensign smoked heroin well into the night. Bethany had an interesting heroin pipe. It was a hybrid glass marijuana bowl attached to a water chamber. Bethany, same as Ensign, enjoyed crafting her own smoking devices.

As he lay on the bed against the headboard, Bethany straddled Ensign while topless, With only a thong on, and Ensign in his boxer shorts, they shotgunned hits of heroin back and forth to one another. Ensign would hit the pipe, put his mouth to hers, and blow smoke into Bethany's mouth as they kissed passionately. Then Bethany would hit the pipe and do the same to Ensign. Ensign felt his eyelids becoming heavy from the heroin. The hotrails kept him awake, but meth didn't stave off the other effects of the heroin.

As the Sun came up, the car service dropped Ensign off on the street by his Lexus. He unlocked his car and sat down in the driver's seat. Before Ensign could gather up tools to work on the engine, the heroin put him to sleep. Two hours later, Ensign was awake again. Two hotrails after that, and he popped the hood to continue his disassembly of his car's engine.

Dean's mom brought Ensign a cup of coffee. She let Ensign know that breakfast would be served at the table on the back patio in five minutes. Ensign thanked her and went inside to a bathroom to wash up. Ensign walked through the house and out the door to the patio. Dean and his mother were seated at the table.

Ensign sat down in front of his plate. He set his coffee cup next to his orange juice. On his plate, there were eggs, bacon, and toast. The eggs were sunny side up, Ensign's preferred way to have them. He shook some salt and pepper onto the eggs. Ensign passed the pepper to Dean. He then watched Dean do something which changed the way Ensign ate eggs forever going forward.

"Oh, my God…"

"My aunt showed me this when I was a kid. Trust me, I've done this my whole life."

"Really?"

"Yes, try it."

"Alright, I'll give it a shot."

Dean handed the pepper back to Ensign. Dean looked at Ensign and raised his eyebrows. Ensign smiled. He took the shaker and completely covered his eggs with a black layer of pepper. When Ensign took a bite, he tasted what had been missing from breakfast every morning. It was as if he had discovered a new food. In that moment, Ensign was converted.

Crystal Clear

For the next week, Ensign's focus remained on disassembling his engine, replacing parts, and rebuilding it. Ensign took breaks in the daytime to go do things with Unique. Dean and Ensign took time to go to the store, go out to eat, or to get ice cream. At times, Ensign walked, by himself, through the neighborhoods to the auto parts store or the grocery store. Ensign continued to interact with many people online, but he only met up with others in the evenings; once it was dark outside; the lack of light inhibiting his ability to work on his car.

Ensign spent two thousand dollars on the engine parts. He worked hard in the sweltering summer Sun. Ensign walked half a mile back from the auto parts store one day with a bag full of supplies, dragging a new floor jack. He tired himself out. He shed blood and sweat...and he finally finished the repairs...and his car didn't start.

One day, in Dean's basement, Ensign bumped into a pedestal; one which had some pottery artwork on it. The sculpture fell and broke. When Dean arrived home, Ensign told him what happened. He apologized, and he gave Dean a hundred dollars to make amends.

Ensign wished he could have given more money to Dean, but his car issues had been depleting his funds at a fast rate. Since he had stepped away from the crystal market, Ensign no longer had a source of incoming income. He was still stranded, and he wasn't sure how he was going to get back on track.

Dean and Ensign had a talk one afternoon. Multiple issues: the broken vase, Dean's fear for his mother's health during the pandemic, all of Ensign's bags and belongings filling up the floorspace in the basement...the two weeks Ensign spent in Dean's basement reached the end. Ensign appreciated the hospitality. He knew he needed to sort out his situation.

Ensign's friend Lex often traveled for work. She built up reward points at hotels...many rewards points. Again, through her help, Ensign had a partial solution to his predicament. Ensign still had other concerns beyond immediate lodging. He had a basement full of belongings at Dean's house, he had a car he fixed but still refused to run, his personal supply of crystal was dwindling down low, and his money had also diminished, leaving him borderline broke.

One problem at a time. With lodging situated, Ensign's next immediate concern was his luggage in Dean's basement. All the bags and items were his most important items; the items he always took when he traveled. His storage unit back in Ohio was completely filled from floor to high ceiling, wall to wall. Over the couple of years of travel, items were picked from storage to accompany Ensign on trips, while other items were taken out from his car and packed into storage. Ensign fine-tuned his travel items to what was needed, what was valuable, what was important to him, and what was useful as he traveled the country.

Though his Lexus trunk and back seats had been packed completely full of his travel items while he traveled, Ensign knew it wasn't smart to reload his belongings from Dean's basement into a broken-down car on the side of the road. It wasn't just his concern for theft while his car sat unoccupied on a street, away from his current physical location. A big concern was the possibility Ensign would come back to his car one day to find it had been towed: all his belongings gone with the car.

"First month; only one dollar. Reserve online now. Move in immediately."

The ad had him with; "First month; only one dollar." With fees and taxes, it became; "First month; fifty-seven dollars." Ensign was desperate, though. He made it happen. He had to pull the trigger in a timely fashion. Ensign confirmed the rental as he sat on a chair outside of the restaurant in his hotel's parking lot. It was sunny and hot outside. Ensign was four miles from Dean's house. He had three of his bags with him: a backpack, a travel bag with a shoulder strap, and a roller suitcase. Since he reserved a storage unit, Ensign decided to walk the four miles, through Aurora, back to the basement where the rest of his belongings were waiting for him.

Ensign had walked much of the Aurora area during the night when the Sun was down. That four-mile daytime walk back to Dean's house was challenging. It was midday, the Sun was bright, and the temperature was in the high nineties. Ensign's backpack and shoulder bag weighed him down. His suitcase caught issue with any bump or curb as he walked.

Ensign stopped in the back of a parking lot to rest. A car pulled into a parking space along the side of the building where Ensign was sitting. Besides the car and him, that section in the back of the parking lot was void of people; or so he thought. The two thug-looking guys in the car noticed Ensign seated on the pavement with his luggage. They stared in his direction. Ensign nodded back in their direction.

To Ensign's surprise, a third guy walked out from around the corner of the building a few feet away from him. He walked right past Ensign, toward the parked car. That guy's gun was sticking out of the back of his waistband. Ensign's gun was in plain view in the holster on his ankle. The third guy glanced in Ensign's direction before stepping into the back seat of the parked car.

Ensign casually averted his gaze and scanned the rest of the parking lot. He remained seated on the cement when the third guy stepped back out of the car and put something in his pocket. As the car with the two guys backed out of the parking space and pulled away, the third guy walked by Ensign; back behind the building from which he had emerged five minutes earlier. Ensign decided his break was over. He gathered his bags, and he continued on towards Dean's house. Ensign felt it was no longer an option to remain seated on that curb.

Ensign first noticed it on the nights he was out wandering the Aurora streets. He noticed it more clearly during that daytime walk through the city. Aurora was laid out like no city he had experienced before. Ensign found no rhyme or reason to the organization of the city. The neighborhoods appeared to have been dropped randomly in place. Streets branched off in odd angles and curves from each other. Demographics, housing developments, business districts; they all sprawled out seemingly haphazardly and random. Arbitrary business areas and neighborhoods were placed directly adjacent to unmatching non-complimentary locales.

From Ensign's experience, cities tended to have organization. From details such as standard street grids and gradual increases or decreases of classiness, most cities made sense in Ensign's mind. Aurora, on the other hand, appeared to just be built outward by whomever, in no particular pattern, with no particular plan. Ensign had no way of knowing what to expect on each block until he reached the next block over. He took in all the sights as he worked his way through the city. Traffic was heavy. Congestion was widespread. Aurora was alive and bustling during the pandemic.

Ensign had Dean pull his FJ Cruiser up to the front of the lot. Ensign punched the code into the keypad by the main doors of the structure. He came back out to Dean's car, wheeling a large, flat cart. Ensign thanked Dean for his help as they finished loading all his luggage onto the cart. Ensign let Dean know he would take it from there. He pushed the cart into the elevator, and he ascended three floors up the warehouse to the floor where he rented a five-by-five-foot storage unit.

After unloading all his items in a manner which allowed easiest access to the items which he would need the most access, Ensign was left with a small floor space in front of the door. He closed the door and shut himself inside the cramped space.

Through the thin metal walls of the structure, Ensign heard other people loading and unloading items into their units all around him. He heard conversations clearly in close proximity.

Ensign made sure his door was securely shut on the inside by wedging a screwdriver along the door's track. He unpacked his bag of drug supplies in the semi-darkness. When he determined there wasn't another person in the immediate vicinity of his storage locker, when the closest voices he heard came from a separate hallway, Ensign fired up the torch and blew down a hotrail. He blew the smoke into a balled-up sweatshirt. Most of the smoke was absorbed, but some dissipated into the air in his tight quarters. Ensign placed the sweatshirt on one side of the open floorspace.

Even if the unit had been completely empty, the floor was only five feet by five feet of space. Since it was filled with all his travel luggage on both sides of the door, Ensign had to curl up and wedge himself into the tight available floor space. Six hours later, one of Ensign's extra-loud snores woke him up. He laughed as he thought about any of the other people using the storage unit who may have heard snoring coming from a unit adjacent to their own.

Alexithymia

Some nights, Ensign stayed in hotels. Others, he had a reclining lawn chair, with blankets and pillows, set up on Dean's back patio. On those nights, Ensign slept under the stars. He had electricity from the house to keep his phones and battery packs charged. Dean's mom brought him coffee each morning. They ate breakfast outside at the table on the patio. Ensign used the downstairs bathroom to shower when needed. He tattooed himself in the backyard under the Sun.

One night, as he lay under the stars, Ensign began interacting with a guy from an app. The guy was a good-looking Mexican guy, in Denver on a construction job. He had a temporary apartment for the duration of his construction contract. Through broken English on their phone call, the twenty-eight-year-old Mexican guy told Ensign two things; Jesus told Ensign he wanted to come pick him up for the night, and he expressed how he wanted Ensign to tattoo him.

Jesus did crystal. Ensign didn't bring any of his own along to Jesus's apartment. Ensign was at the very end of his supply. Jesus had a glass pipe with about a gram of crystal melted into the glass bowl. The quality was low, but Ensign was in no position to complain that night.

Ensign tattooed a band of random colors and designs around Jesus's right calf. During intervals of tattooing, Jesus needed breaks from the pain of the needle. Crystal smoking and intimacy filled time until Jesus was ready for more ink. It was light outside the next morning when the tattoo was finished. Ensign let Jesus decide how much to pay him for the tattoo.

Jesus then dropped Ensign off on the main street close to Dean's neighborhood, at the large grocery store in the strip mall.

Ensign came out of the store with chicken wings and bleu cheese dressing. He sat on a cement parking block to eat, since all the tables and benches close to the store were chained off due to pandemic restrictions. Ensign looked around through the parking lots and businesses to all the commotion and people on foot moving all around the area. Ensign was in an extremely traffic-congested, busy section of Aurora.

When he finished eating, Ensign crossed the grocery store parking lot to place his garbage in a receptacle outside the gas station, close to the main street. Ensign walked out to the sidewalk in front of the gas station. Dean's neighborhood was across the main thoroughfare. Ensign walked down the sidewalk to join the congregation of pedestrians waiting for the traffic light to change at the corner crosswalk.

Eventually, the light changed, and the signal indicated it was safe to walk across the street. Ensign walked into the street, following immediately behind two college-aged girls. He had only reached the middle of the six lanes of traffic when the signal changed, indicating it was no longer safe to walk. As he picked up to a jog to make it across the three remaining lanes of traffic, Ensign felt something. He knew what it was, and a flash of panic washed through him.

All the backed-up traffic at the intersection began to move at once. Ensign froze for only a second, then he made a quick decision to run to safety on the opposite side of the road. As he ran, Ensign felt something else. He hoped he would make it across without feeling what he felt. It didn't work out that way. Ensign looked back as he jumped to the safety of the sidewalk on the far side of the street. He looked back and saw what he knew he would see. He watched the ground where heavy traffic had begun speeding across the intersection in both directions.

During Ensign's travels around the country, people gave him random gifts they wished him to have. Prior to his trip out West,

Ensign was given a gift from someone when he spent a night at a house in South Bend, Indiana. Though that situation was odd on many levels, Ensign very much used the gift he had been given when he left the house.

As he looked out into that busy intersection, Ensign watched that particular gift roll on the pavement and come to a stop in the exact middle of the intersection. As Ensign continued to watch, wondering what he was going to do, a Cadillac Escalade ran over the heavy-duty silicone cock ring which had slipped off his cock and balls and rolled down to the bottom of his pant leg as he crossed the crosswalk.

Before Ensign could lift his foot up to grab it, while it momentarily rested atop his shoe under his pantleg, he felt the cock ring roll from off his ankle, out of his pant leg, and into the intersection. That moment was the exact moment when all traffic began driving through the intersection when the light changed. That was the very instant Ensign needed to immediately run to finish crossing the intersection.

When the Cadillac Escalade ran over the ring, the back wheel sent it into the air. Ensign watched, in what seemed to be slow motion, as the ring landed back in the crosswalk. Cars blew by it for the next minute, but no other cars ran it over. The light eventually changed again, and the signal cleared people to walk again at the crosswalk.

Ensign was ready. At the moment the signal gave him clearance, he ran at full speed across three of the lanes of traffic. He quickly reached down to the pavement as he pivoted and positioned to sprint back to the side of the road. Ensign missed the grab. He went down again and succeeded in snatching the cock ring from the road. Ensign ran back across, and he caught his breath as he walked on into the neighborhoods leading to Dean's house.

Ensign's faith in that cock ring remained solid. Though it had been run over, there was no damage to the silicone's integrity. Though it was dirty from the tires and the pavement, it remained fully useable. Ensign washed it once he got back to Dean's house, and he put it back in its rightful location…around his cock and balls.

The Golden Ratio

Gun laws in Colorado were interesting. As long as Ensign wasn't within the city limits of Denver, he was legally able to open carry his handgun. His ankle holster was preferred. It became an issue on particularly hot days. Sweat from his leg required Ensign to move his gun to the alternate leg. Sometimes, he would just take the holster off and wipe the sweat from his leg.

Ensign stopped when he reached the far side of an overpass one day as he walked through the city. He adjusted his gun on his leg. He was in an unfamiliar section of Aurora. Like the areas he knew, it was busy with traffic and people everywhere. Cars filled the traffic lanes on the roads; the stopped traffic was backed up in all directions when the stoplights were red. The sea of cars in parking lots filled in all but a select few spaces.

There was a convenience store, a busy oasis in the parking lot of a large section of strip mall businesses. People were all over, walking in and out of the stores, including the convenience store which caught Ensign's attention. All the gas pumps were occupied with vehicles, and some pumps had small lines of cars waiting for their turn to fuel. Ensign managed to run across two intersections of congestion to reach the store.

Reminding Ensign of the rest stop when he first arrived in Wyoming weeks earlier, there was another particularly loud and opinionated vagrant yelling from the median of one of the intersections. This guy took it up a notch. He began alternating between yelling and singing at top volume. Ensign also noticed, as he walked into the store, the guy began taking off his clothes.

Ensign did a hotrail in the bathroom of the store. He came out and purchased ice cream. Ensign walked outside again to sit at a picnic table and eat ice cream with a plastic spoon. Ensign stood up when the then almost fully naked singer approached the table where he was sitting. As Ensign stood up from the table, still eating his ice cream, the guy, still yelling and singing, stopped walking in his direction.

He froze for a second as he looked Ensign up and down. He didn't make a sound. It was the only time the guy had been quiet since Ensign first walked from the overpass into that section of the city. Ensign nodded to him. Then, as if his silent trance had been broken, the guy spun around to walk back to the road. The singing and yelling resumed at full volume.

A few blocks later, on Ensign's walk, police swarmed an apartment complex with sirens on. As Ensign shuffled down the sidewalk between the parking lot of the apartments and the road, other people across the street got into a fight. Ensign sat down on a bus stop bench after he walked another half mile. He needed to rest. The Sun had almost completely set, but the temperature was still hot. Ensign was in another area he hadn't before been…somewhere between his hotel room and his storage unit. More emergency vehicles flew by in the traffic, lights and sirens blazing. Ensign had four miles left to walk.

The Sun went down completely. It was night, and Ensign found himself in a creepy back alley; one with graffiti on the buildings and broken beer bottles all over the ground. Around a corner, there was a pile of tires, ten feet tall. In the center, a door to what appeared to be an abandoned trailer. The lock was broken off, and the door was cracked open. Ensign saw only black as he tried to look into the crack of the door.

From where he was standing, Ensign could see both directions down the alleys. The ways out of the alleys were both well over a hundred yards in different directions from where he wandered. He had been distracted looking at his phone when he drifted much farther from the streets, traffic, and people than he would have; had he been paying attention. He was alone, or so he thought. He listened to the silence. Then, Ensign heard a noise behind him in the shadows. He heard another noise from inside the trailer amongst the tires.

Ensign wasn't sure if it was paranoia from a sleep-deprived and drug-saturated brain, or if his sudden sense of urgency was due to a real threat. Ensign chose to reach down and remove his handgun from the ankle holster. He picked the direction away from where he had entered the alleys, and he began to walk between the buildings. He could see cars passing on a street, far up in the distance.

Ensign stayed alert as he walked, scanning all directions in the darkness. He made sure to pass by the completely dark and shadowed corners of the alley as far to the opposite side as he could walk. There was complete silence as Ensign made his way closer to the main street, still far up in the distance. Eventually, as he got closer, Ensign began to hear the traffic driving by on the main road.

Ensign stayed vigilant while he closed the distance between the depths of that shadowy, isolated corridor and the bustling civilization back in the heavy traffic of Aurora's streets. Ensign stopped recording video and put his phone back in his pocket. Before stepping back from between the buildings and out to the sidewalk, Ensign put his gun back in his ankle holster.

Ensign continued on his walk through the city, and he vowed to himself to remain on those surface streets the rest of that night. He knew he still had a couple of miles to walk. He was hot and tired, but he chose not to take any more routes away from the main roads as a shortcut. Ensign crossed paths with other random people, and with groups of others out in the Aurora night, but his paranoia subsided once he was back in public areas.

Ensign was alone as he walked, but that feeling he had when he was deep in that alley was beyond alone. He wasn't sure what those noises were that he heard in the depths of that darkness. He hadn't stuck around to find out. The noises could have been the sounds of small animals rummaging for food. The noises could have been something else entirely. Ensign was perfectly fine, knowing he would never know.

Rainbow Ridge

Dean ran an extension cord from a power outlet on his house to Ensign's car on the street. There were nights when Ensign wasn't in a hotel, where Ensign chose to sleep in his car instead of sleeping in the open air of Dean's back patio. Some nights, the weather wasn't conducive to sleeping outside. On those nights, the extension cord from Dean's house, plugged into a power strip inside his car, charged Ensign's phone and powered his tattoo equipment. The cord also powered a small nightlight and Ensign's small desk fan.

Ensign's arms became heavily tattooed during his time in Colorado. Ensign had again been using crystal intravenously, at a more consistent rate, while he was out West. He tattooed himself strategically to camouflage his needle use. In the crease of Ensign's left arm, the vein he used most for injections, he tattooed a large blue and black design. He filled it in completely. From that point on, nobody could tell that he had been shooting drugs.

For the first time, since Ensign first began using crystal in the spring of 2017, his supply was almost diminished. When he decided to leave the game and head west, Ensign procured enough crystal for time he thought was needed. He hadn't anticipated becoming stranded in Colorado.

When Ensign first reached Colorado earlier in the summer, his supply for personal use dropped below an ounce. Though he had never had under an ounce at any point in the previous three years, he wasn't concerned. His car was still running fine. Soon after, his car broke down. Ensign's supply continued to dwindle away. After two weeks of working on the engine and changing parts, Ensign's car remained immobile. His crystal supply continued to dissipate, closer and closer to nothing.

Ensign needed to sort out his situation. He reached out to Unique. She made something happen to help him out. At about four in the afternoon one day, while Ensign sat in his broken-down car, an SUV pulled up behind him on the street. Ensign stepped from his driver's seat and walked back to his trunk. A blonde, White, younger guy, who looked to be college aged, stepped from the SUV. He walked to meet Ensign on the street at the back of his car. Ensign extended his hand in greeting. They shook hands. The blonde guy asked Ensign a question.

"How do you want to do this?"

"The amount Unique told me is right there in the trunk next to the speaker box. Drop it there when you pick up the money."

The whole exchange took thirty seconds. The guy got back in his car and drove away. Ensign stayed back at his trunk for another couple minutes and worked on the speakers in case any nosey neighbors happened to be minding his business. Ensign then took the brown rolled-up lunch bag and put it in his pocket.

Ensign walked back to his driver's seat and quickly got on his phone to secure a ride service to somewhere else. Once again, he had more than an ounce of crystal. The anxiety of his supply running out was relieved when Ensign got high while he waited for the car to pick him up. Ensign then had a new anxiety as he waited to leave the scene where a blatant drug transaction had just occurred.

The car from the ride service dropped Ensign off at an apartment complex in inner-city Denver. Ensign had been interacting with a Mexican trans girl. They had been communicating using a translation app. Ensign spoke no Spanish, and she didn't speak a word of English. They knew they wouldn't be doing any talking upon Ensign's arrival. As he walked up to the appropriate apartment, Ensign wondered how the intimacy was going to go down without any verbal communication. He was high, and he looked forward to the challenge.

It proved to be no challenge at all. The girl took Ensign's hand after she opened the door. She led him through her apartment to her bedroom. She motioned him to her bed, and they both removed their clothes. After they finished, they kissed, and Ensign walked back outside to wait for the next car to pick him up. It was nighttime when he walked out to the road from the apartment. Two minutes after he reached the curb, a car pulled up and stopped in front of him. Ensign got in, and they pulled away from the complex.

Unique put Ensign in touch with her uncle. He was a mechanic in Denver. He offered Ensign help. He planned to meet Ensign at his Lexus to see if he could figure out why his car wouldn't start. Unique's uncle told Ensign that if he wasn't able to get his car to run, he would be able to find him a reasonably priced car to buy. Ensign happily accepted his help, and they set up a day and time for Unique's uncle to come look at his car.

Though Ensign's car's engine wouldn't turn over, it still cranked when he pushed the button to start it. Unique's uncle showed Ensign something when he attempted to start the car. He showed Ensign where to place his hand on the engine when he pushed the button for the ignition. Unique's uncle asked if Ensign felt it. He told Ensign what it was he felt each time he attempted to turn over the engine.

Ensign felt, and heard, the knocking in the engine. Ensign had blown his head gasket. Unique's uncle explained to Ensign how he would need to find another engine if he wished to ever drive his car again. He explained how Ensign would be better off finding another car. He told Ensign he would locate something for him if he wished to buy another car. Ensign gave Unique's uncle a price range, thanked him for his time, and told him to let him know what he could find.

Dean came out of his house to talk to Ensign as Unique's uncle was leaving. Ensign told him his bad news. Dean told Ensign he had a good friend who was also a mechanic. He told Ensign he would reach out to his friend to see if he could come out for a second opinion. Later that day, Dean told Ensign his mechanic would be over in two days.

Dean's mechanic friend, like the trans girl from the week before, didn't speak a word of English. Dean functioned as translator between his friend and Ensign. After an hour of inspection, adjustments, and translated conversation, Ensign was informed of the same conclusion by Dean's mechanic friend which Unique's uncle had told him two days before. Again, Ensign's heart sank. His car was dead, and it was stuck there on the side of the road…and Ensign lost any hope he could fix it and continue on his westward journey through the country.

Later, after being over at an internet hookup's house, Ensign arrived back at his car at three in the morning. He was tired, and he looked forward to closing himself up in his car and getting some sleep. Ensign pushed the unlock button on his key fob to unlock his car doors…it didn't work. He tried again…it didn't work. He tried his keys in the door handles…that didn't work either.

After twenty minutes, and a futile effort, Ensign called to get more use out of his auto club membership, the membership Lex bought him when his car first died on the side of the highway. Ensign waited outside in the dark and fog for another hour. He became more impatient and frustrated the more tired he grew.

As Ensign struggled to keep his eyes open, a tow truck showed up. As had been done at that park in Minnesota, an inflatable airbag was used to separate the car window from its frame. A metal rod reached the door handle of the opposite door. A hook on the end pulled the handle, and the door popped open. Ensign thanked the serviceman. The sky had just begun to turn from black to purple, indicating dawn was approaching. He didn't know it at the time, but Ensign had just used up his yearly service calls included with his membership. Ensign, once in his car, succumbed to much needed sleep.

Black Swan

"We are all the black swans we are trying to avoid."

Ensign rode with Unique in the middle of the night. They headed from Aurora to her house in Denver. A conversation began; one which seemed familiar. Unique brought up something which reminded Ensign of that night when he vowed to never again travel to Troy, Michigan. Ensign wasn't the originator of the conversation. Ensign spent that time in Unique's car listening to her speak. Unique brought up the topic, and Ensign purposely refrained from adding anything from his perspective.

Ensign listened, he acknowledged, and he allowed Unique to share what was on her mind. Ensign wanted her to take the conversation where she wished it to go. Ensign wanted to hear all the similarities with prior conversations he'd had previously; in another part of the country with a person Unique didn't even know existed. Back when he was in Lansing, Simon and Ensign had begun their discussions of the same topic. Without prompt, Unique spoke of the exact same things that Simon and Ensign had already discussed.

On that drive with Unique, Ensign felt the conversation was too accurate to be shared drug paranoia. Unique spoke of those who watch the chosen people. She told Ensign, (prior to Ensign ever mentioning the cars driving along with him to Troy, Michigan) that if he paid attention, he would be able to identify the watchers. Unique told Ensign that a white SUV played a role in the scenario...and that was when Ensign could hold his tongue no longer.

Ensign shared with Unique what happened to him which made him avoid Troy, Michigan. Unique took it in stride. Their weird conversation continued to get weirder as Unique drove them through the night. They both seemed to know and understand what each other was saying. Ensign tried his hardest to blame their conversation on their use of crystal; the similarities, and their thoughts, lined up too perfectly to be just the drugs. It felt as if the two of them were selected to know what only certain people were to ever find out. It felt as if something bigger had let a secret slip. Ensign wanted it to be the drugs. It was an eerie feeling. Ensign didn't think it was the drugs...

Their conversation continued as they sat in Unique's car on the street outside her house. It was the middle of the night. The neighborhood was quiet and dark. There were cars parked randomly on the street. Unique's neighborhood, unlike neighborhoods in Aurora, was a grid of square blocks; streets crossing each other at perpendicular angles. Unique's house was on the corner of two of the streets.

They had parked on the street next to Unique's house, facing into the neighborhood from the outskirts. There were streetlights, one on each side of the road, one on each block. From where they were parked, Ensign saw all the way into the neighborhood. In the distance, directly ahead of him, Ensign saw where that street ended: the main road on the opposite side of the neighborhood. Ensign saw where the intersecting cross streets met the street where they had parked, incrementally along their street, down to the far side of the neighborhood. They were the only people out in the dark depths of night.

Suddenly, an hour after they first parked to talk, they both stopped talking. Unique and Ensign shared a glance at each other in that moment of silence. Ensign had a bad feeling. He could tell Unique had a bad feeling, as well. They both listened carefully in the night. Their car windows were down. Until that moment, the two of them heard nothing in the silence but their own conversation. They didn't speak. They both heard it. It was coming closer. They whispered to each other.

"What is it?"

"I don't know, but it's coming."

"Get as low as you can in your seat..."

Ensign slid down as low as he could get while still being able to see over the dashboard. It was coming fast. It sounded like it was coming from a side street, two streets up on the right...and that was exactly where he first saw it. As the screeching of the tires and roar of the engine broke through, the car slid out into the road, two streets up from where Unique had parked her car. The car skidded around the corner to face them and accelerate in their direction.

From where he was, Ensign saw two silhouettes in the front seats of the dark sedan. Under the streetlight, Ensign clearly saw the third person; he was out of the window of the back door, seated in the space of the rolled-down window. On his face; a wild-eyed stare. In his hand; a gun. Ensign watched, once the car completed the turn two blocks up from them.

"Is that a gun?"

"Yes, get down."

The engine roared, as the driver accelerated. The car sped up and drove directly at the car parked a block in front of Unique and Ensign. At the last second, the car pulled back to the center of the road. It flew past that parked car. Again, the driver accelerated directly toward the next parked car on the next block; Unique's car, where Unique and Ensign were both watching as they were slumped down in the front seats.

Again...at the last second, the driver swerved back from hitting Unique's car directly head-on. They cut back into the middle of the road to rip past them. Unique and Ensign were both frozen. It all happened so fast; they couldn't react. Ensign hadn't even been able to fully duck down in the seat. He just watched as the car with the guy hanging out of the side window flew by them and kept driving. A second later, the tires screeched again as the car turned out of the neighborhood behind them. Ensign heard the engine fade off into the night as the car sped off.

In his mind, Ensign kept that image of the guy with the gun as they narrowly passed them by. His eyes, wide and crazy, seemed to focus on nothing as he stared ahead into the night. His body swayed each time the car swerved toward and away from the parked cars on the street. The gun in his hand, the noises coming from the car's tires and engine, the sheer instant chaos which broke through that silent night in that empty neighborhood... Unique and Ensign snapped out of it. They both knew they urgently needed to get away from there.

Coprophagy

Ensign had a friend for a decade back in Ohio who mostly spent his time as a guy, but sometimes he would live as a girl. Until Ensign first met him, he had never known anyone to split their time between genders. When Ensign reached Colorado, he met someone else online who also lived that way. When Ensign became stranded in Colorado, they made plans to meet.

Ensign had a hotel room situated between Aurora and Denver. Damian knocked on the door while Ensign was in the middle of tattooing himself. Ensign put the tattoo equipment away, and Damian and Ensign began heavy drug use. They made some videos that first night. The next day, they walked through the city to another hotel. The two of them stayed two nights in the second hotel, and then Ensign decided he needed to make a change.

Ensign thought back to the day before; when he used a ride service to travel from the hotel in Aurora to Unique's uncle's auto shop in Denver, then back to Aurora. The trip cost fifty dollars each way. If Ensign rented a car, the car would cost that much per day. The rental made sense.

While Ensign was at Unique's uncle's auto shop, Unique's uncle showed him an SUV he was willing to sell for a decent price. He told Ensign he was going to give the SUV a tune-up for him, and make sure the car had no issues before he bought it. He told Ensign it would take about two weeks. Ensign had forgotten he was within the city limits of Denver when he was at the auto shop, but nobody called him out for open carrying his gun on his ankle.

Damian's sister picked up Damian and Ensign from the hotel and brought them back to her apartment. Ensign made some phone calls. A car service took Damian and Ensign to the Denver airport. After Ensign filled out the proper paperwork, the two of them loaded into the rental car and left for the city. Ensign rented the car for the following week. He was mobile again. He figured it was cheaper than constantly using ride services.

Damian and Ensign were on the highway loop one afternoon in Denver rush hour traffic. The roads in Denver were beyond congested during peak hours. All lanes of traffic were packed on the highways. All exit ramps were backed up. Many stoplights required waiting through multiple cycles of light changes before passing through the intersections.

Damian and Ensign were engaged in a conversation like those he had previously shared with Unique and Simon. That conversation though, Ensign knew the drugs were a key factor. Damian also believed there were "watchers' who tracked him in all he did. His reason was specific; in his mind, he was a demon sent to Earth from another dimension. While Damian tried to convince Ensign that he spoke truth, Ensign began to feel Damian was more unhinged with each word.

Ensign's GPS map wasn't displaying a correct route to get through the city. After a half hour of frustrating driving, Ensign ended up looping around and stopping at the same red light which they had stopped a half hour earlier. Ensign's patience was wearing thin. Damian noticed, and he took the opportunity to try to make Ensign angry. Anytime Ensign said anything, Damian replied abrasively; seeking to get a rise out of Ensign.

"Oh man...we were just at this light a half an hour ago."

"You don't know how to read the map."

"Yes, I do. I showed you how it looped us back around."

"Nope. It's you. You don't know what you are doing."

"Seriously? I don't have the patience for this..."

"It's you. You can't read the map."

"Dude...I'm serious. I'll drop you off on the side of this highway..."

The stop-and-go traffic was unrelenting. The negative replies to everything Ensign said became as frustrating as the traffic. Their words escalated and became more heated. Damian was trying to get under Ensign's skin. It worked. Five minutes later, Ensign pulled to the shoulder at the top of a busy overpass. As he slammed on the breaks, Damian flung open his car door and jumped out to the road. Ensign drove forward in the slow traffic. He saw Damian in his mirror. Damian walked down the side of the overpass to the road below. Ensign shook his head while he drove away.

Once he pulled into the parking lot at his storage unit a half hour later, Ensign checked his phone. He called Damian, and Damian picked up. Ensign apologized for his role in the escalation of their conversation, and he offered to swing back into the city and pick up Damian. Damian apologized as well. He told Ensign he wanted to see how mad he was able to make him. Ensign told him he could be back that way in thirty minutes. Damian politely declined.

When he hung up, Ensign saw he had a few messages from someone on one of the apps. The guy was a younger-looking Asian. He lived on his family's farm outside Boulder, Colorado. He wanted Ensign to come over at one o'clock in the morning. Ensign agreed to visit, and he went up into his storage unit to sort out some items.

At one o'clock in the morning, Ensign managed to find the family farm, off of a highway close to Boulder, Colorado. Ensign pulled in and waited. Moments later, the guy came out to his car. He directed Ensign to park on the side of a barn in the front yard and turn off the car. Ensign was told those instructions were necessary because the guy's parents and siblings were asleep in the house. The two of them spent the next few hours attempting to make quiet videos while sweating all over the inside of Ensign's rental car.

The Exception

After the time stranded in the metro Denver area, Ensign again felt freedom as he drove south from Colorado Springs. He visited Stacey again in Pueblo. He spent another day in Trinidad after stopping for the night in southern Colorado. He recorded the sunset from a field at the foot of the Rocky Mountains. Ensign continued ignoring texts from Justin as he passed into northern New Mexico. Ensign was again out on the roads; enjoying the sense of freedom he felt behind the wheel of the rental car.

Ensign did drugs in parking lots, and at scenic overlooks. He met new people on his phone. Some plans materialized; others fell through. Ensign showered at truck stops. He updated friends with status reports. He took time in his car, and in the shower rooms of truck stops, to video-interact with intimate online partners. At random intervals, Ensign tattooed himself along the way. He explored new locations. He did his best to leave all of his immediate concerns on the side of the road back in Aurora. Ensign knew, in those rental car moments, he needed to live… and he needed to appreciate that fleeting feeling in life; that which comes from magical experiences.

Ensign was living it up on borrowed (rented) time. When that first week with the car ended, he extended his rental for a second week. Unique's uncle hadn't finished his work on the SUV, so Ensign opted for more time with the rental car. He was approaching the end of that second week, and he knew time was becoming a concern. Having the freedom to travel as he wished, he didn't want it to end.

Unique's uncle told Ensign that he found a pinhole leak in the transmission housing of the SUV. He told Ensign his options; he could take it as-is; risking a breakdown, or Ensign could hold off until Unique's uncle could find the time to attempt a repair. Unique's uncle wasn't sure when he was going to be able to work on the car, and Ensign's car rental fees were adding up quickly over time.

A woman from the website had been in contact with Ensign since well before he began traveling out West. Her name, in the real world, was Gina. According to her profile name, the info in her profile, and her messages; she was a lesbian seeking only women. She had been the one to reach out first. She had been the one initially pursuing a dynamic. She had been the one, once she learned of Ensign's plans to head across the country in her direction, who insisted Ensign make a stop to see her.

"You're interested in me? According to your profile, you specifically seek women."

"Yes, but you're the exception. There's just something about you…"

The exception: Ensign always seemed to be the exception. He didn't particularly enjoy being the exception. It gave him an odd feeling; one which made him wonder if the novelty of his looks and personality would wear off when what was sought wasn't who he was. Age, race, gender, body type, even tattoo coverage… Ensign was always someone's exception to their previously stated desires and turn-on/turn-offs. Was he a trophy? Was he an experiment? Was he a placeholder to fill time until they found what they were actually seeking? It gave Ensign a sense of loneliness. It also gave him a feeling which convinced him he was a temporary fix for whatever it was that was missing from other people's lives.

Though Ensign knew that most of his interactions, once brought into the real world, were temporary or one-time occurrences, he also wasn't happy knowing there was a glass ceiling on the extent of the intimacy which wasn't within his control. Ensign never wished to force anything which wasn't meant to happen. Being the exception; it caused him to feel the end from the beginning. As the exception, Ensign felt he was set up for failure.

Gina lived in Littleton, Colorado. She was in the process of moving to a new apartment during the weekend Ensign agreed to meet her. That Friday evening, Ensign pulled into the parking lot near the soccer fields of Columbine High School. He left from a friend's house a few miles away. On his way to Columbine, Ensign saw something which made him drive back and forth on a certain road multiple times to record video. That side of the Denver metro area had much less traffic and congestion than most of the other areas, so it was easy to drive by and record video.

What Ensign saw was a house. It was unlike any he had ever seen. The house was by itself on a large lot on the side of a main road through the area. The house was huge. It seemed as if the builder had no limits of money or to their artistic fantasies. Ensign took some time to search for the house online, and he eventually found it. The house had been built by the owner of a construction company, and there was a controversy in the city involving delays on completion. It was yet another random fact; information which never would have entered his brain had Ensign not happened to drive down that particular road.

Once he was satisfied with his internet search for the house, Ensign stepped from his car to walk down to the lake adjacent from the Columbine High School grounds. In the late afternoon, the Sun began to set. The reflection of the pink and purple clouds on the clear mirror lake surface was as beautiful as the sky itself. The pristine calm of the water was only disturbed by random families of ducks swimming in the water. It was a wonderful place for Ensign to collect his thoughts and record video of an amazing natural scene. Ensign was at peace during that moment in his life, however briefly that moment was set to last...

A Dull Ache

When he got up to leave, after spending the weekend with Gina, Ensign checked his phone. He had a reminder text from the airport car rental company. It was Sunday. Ensign's car was due back on Monday. He made up his mind in that moment. He wasn't going to return the car on Monday. He still needed to drive the rental car until Unique's uncle was ready with the SUV.

Two things happened on Tuesday of that following week: the rental car company billed Ensign an additional nine hundred dollars...and the deal with Unique's uncle fell through. Ensign called the rental car company. He told them he was going to keep the car for another full week since they billed him an additional week's price. He wasn't worried about another bill from them. They had already taken the last of the money in his bank account. Ensign was worried about the SUV no longer being an option. His time in Colorado reached a new level of desperation.

Ensign was basically out of money. While he had the rental car, he had to jump back in the game to make cash to survive. Ensign had most of that ounce of crystal from Unique's friend. He thought it was going to be exclusively for personal use, but he had to improvise due to the recent changes. A few of Ensign's friends sent him money upon hearing the update regarding his situation.

Ensign let go of insignificant amounts of crystal here and there, but it wasn't enough to cover living expenses. He decided he would turn the car back in at the airport the following Sunday when the rental company was closed. Unique had agreed to follow Ensign to drop the car off, and then she would give him a ride back from the airport. They planned to drop the car off in the middle of the night. Ensign still had a couple more days to drive.

Ensign went down to Pueblo that first night to see Stacey one more time. He returned to Dean's house the next morning. Ensign was putting in as many miles as he could. It was past the middle of September, and Ensign was still in Colorado. He thought he would have checked Oregon off from his travel list by then. Instead, Ensign realized he wasn't going to be checking Oregon off the list at all.

Ensign spent the afternoon setting up a donation page on social media. He posted about it on other social media outlets. Ensign set up the page to receive enough donations to buy a car and head away from Colorado. He decided he needed to consolidate his two storage units. Ensign needed a car which was big enough to fit everything from his Colorado storage unit as well as all the parts he could strip from his Lexus before he left it on the street. Ensign planned to drive everything back to his larger (and much fuller) storage unit in Ohio. From there, he would have some breathing room to sort out his next moves.

Around midnight that night, Ensign met someone from a social media app. In the middle of the night, Ensign picked up the Mexican trans girl from a neighborhood close to downtown Denver. It was late. It was dark outside. Nowhere was open, and they couldn't hang out at her place. Her family was all home.

Taylor told Ensign that she had an idea. She told him to drive, and she would direct him to where they were going to go. Ensign headed west towards the outskirts of Denver; to the side of the city where the eastern slopes of the Rocky Mountains began. The two of them headed up into the mountains west of Denver. As dawn broke, Taylor and Ensign ascended Lookout Mountain. They stopped at an overlook to watch the Sun rise over the Denver metro area. It was beautiful. Taylor was beautiful, the morning sunlight, a perfect backdrop.

That morning, Taylor told Ensign she was going to take him to one more location before they found a hotel. Ensign drove them through Golden, Colorado and further into the mountain towns west of Denver. They reached Morrison, Colorado. The Sun was bright in the morning sky.

Ensign stopped in the middle of the road to let three deer casually cross in front of them. They were at Red Rocks Amphitheatre. Ensign was in awe. He thanked Taylor for her guidance. Ensign let her know how happy he was to share that once in a lifetime experience with her that morning. The two of them came down out of the mountains, and Ensign used his phone to find a hotel once they were back in Golden.

Though Taylor and Ensign shared intimacy in the hotel room that day, Ensign was a disappointment. The drugs didn't allow him to fully perform in the way he had hoped. He felt bad about it. They slept for a few hours.

When the two of them walked outside to get back in the car, snow covered the ground. They were shocked. It wasn't even the end of September. It was still summer for a few more days. The internet informed them of the record earliest snowfall in Denver.

All Good Things

Again, Ensign's friend Lex saved him. The social media donation page was a success. Ensign made thirty-five hundred dollars in three days. A large chunk of that money came from Lex. The urgency of Ensign's situation cooled down. Though desperation diminished to a level which no longer consumed him, the unseasonable early snowfall reminded Ensign that winter was soon approaching Colorado. Ensign had some money again. He could eat and survive. He still had drugs. He just needed to find a car.

On that last night in the overdue rental car, Ensign drove to the city of Boulder. He parked in a busy parking lot to shoot drugs and interact with Shannon on his phone. The evening progressed, and the Sun set to the West beyond the mountains. The parking lot, no longer full of people shopping and visiting restaurants, began to take on an eerie vibe.

Cars still littered the large parking lot, but Ensign didn't see a single person once the Sun went down. For two hours, Ensign sat alone in his car that evening. He shot crystal one more time and said goodnight to Shannon. Ensign began to think about how he should spend those last few hours with the rental car before Unique followed him to the airport to drop it off.

Ensign was startled as an old guy walked up to his car. He wasn't sure how he had missed seeing him, but he had. The guy looked into Ensign's window. Ensign assumed the guy was about to ask him for money. Ensign made sure his drugs and paraphernalia were out of sight, and he apprehensively rolled down his window. The guy began to speak. His voice was hard to understand, but Ensign managed to catch the message. The guy didn't ask for money. Instead, he warned Ensign of sitting in that particular parking lot too late into the night.

Ensign thanked the guy, and he rolled his window back up to closed. The guy meandered away across the parking lot. A moment later, he disappeared into the distance behind some of the parked cars. Ensign scanned the parking lot. Drug paranoia and sleep deprivation had Ensign on edge again. He noticed movement between cars parked closest to the strip mall far in front of him. Ensign's mind flashed to the Zombocalypse scene on the highway between Louisville, Kentucky and Nashville, Tennessee two years prior.

A shadowy figure moved out into the parking lot from between the cars. Ensign strained his eyes in an attempt to see what was going on up in front of him. Another figure moved from between cars slightly to the left from where the first figure had walked into the lot. Ensign sat and watched. Both figures walked slowly toward each other and crossed over to continue walking in opposite directions. Ensign then thought back to the zombie prostitutes in the middle of the night in the mountains of West Virginia.

Those figures in the Boulder parking lot moved in a comparable way. They too, seemed to be in a trance or a stupor. Ensign could see one was a guy and one was a girl. They hadn't seen him, parked far out into the middle of the parking lot. Ensign didn't feel threatened in any way. He thought about the words which were spoken to him by the guy who appeared outside his car window. Ensign turned on his car, and he left the parking lot. Ensign left Boulder and headed out to meet Unique at the airport. His time in the rental car had reached its limit.

Dark Flow

Ensign was frustrated, but he was almost finished working on his project of the night. Earlier in the day, his glasses had finally broken to a point where they were no longer functional. A couple of weeks prior, Ensign had anticipated the project. Ensign bought a pair of twenty dollar reading glasses at a convenience store.

After some careful and painstaking work, after frustration and tedious activity, Ensign finally managed to finish creating his new glasses. parts of the twenty dollar reading glasses were fused together with his prescription lenses. Ensign's glasses were frameless. The middle part, the piece holding the lenses together, had broken between the nose pieces. Ensign was satisfied; having connected the arms and middle piece of the reading glasses to his lenses.

Ensign had done a good enough job that they looked legit. He had done the job without the luxury of being able to see as he made his new glasses. He breathed a sigh of relief. Ensign sat back in his driver's seat and stared at the shade covering the inside of his windshield. He relaxed, satisfied with his work.

Something startled him as he was sitting there in his car cocoon. Ensign was in his own world when he was closed off in his broken-down car on the side of the road. Ensign instantly felt a threat to his isolation bubble. As he sprang from his seat, he flung open his car door. Ensign was almost instantly standing in the street outside his car. He caught, with vision aided by his new self-made glasses, the last hurried step as the woman got back on the sidewalk and hurried away from his car.

The woman was walking a dog on a leash. She stared straight ahead, away from Ensign as she moved hurriedly away from him down the street. She didn't fool him at all. Ensign knew exactly what she had done and what she was up to. He called her out on it. Ensign was mad. He knew he surprised her. He caught her in the act.

"Hey!"

The woman glanced back and picked up her pace.

"HEY!"

She stopped when he yelled toward her again.

"I know what you're doing. You're out here every night. I saw it the other day, and I know, for a fact, you just checked the door handle on my car. Keep your hands off my car."

"I'm out walking my dog in my neighborhood…"

"And you didn't expect me to be in my car while you're out checking door handles."

The woman began to walk away faster. Ensign remained next to his car.

"I better not catch you doing that again."

Ensign got no response. Ensign texted Dean and told him to come out to his car for a minute. He told Dean to be sure anytime he left his car outside, the doors were always locked. Dean thanked him for the warning. From then on, the woman stayed on the other side of the street when she walked her dog at night.

Garden of Eden

Ensign was wandering amongst the sculptures and flowers in Dean's backyard one morning while on a break from tattooing himself. His phone in his hand was vibrating at a steady pace as he interacted with people online. A message on an app caught his attention. It stood out from the menagerie of generic compliments and sexual harassment.

"I want to cuddle in bed in underwear for the rest of the day with you."

Ensign was receptive instantly. He let Skye know that he needed to be picked up. Skye pulled up in front of Ensign's Lexus. Ensign grabbed his backpack, and he hopped in the car. It was a twenty-minute drive to Skye's apartment complex on the other side of Aurora. The Sun was shining, the sky was blue, and Ensign had that tingly feeling of anticipation. He was looking forward to cuddling. He failed to mention to Skye that he wasn't wearing underwear.

For the following week, Skye and Ensign played house together. They went grocery shopping and cooked food together in the apartment. They ran errands and stayed in bed together. Ensign tattooed both of them. Skye gave Ensign a nice Carhart winter coat. The nights were getting cold in Colorado. The coat was much needed.

When Ensign had stayed in the Littleton/Columbine area with Gina at the end of that summer in 2020, she had given him all kinds of athletic brand tee shirts and some basketball shorts which her ex-boyfriend left with her when he moved out. The shirts were name-brand and basically brand new, but they weren't going to keep him warm when summer ended. The Carhart coat from Skye was much appreciated. Though the days were still hot, the nights were cold.

It was dark on their drive back from Saint Mary's Glacier. Skye wanted to take Ensign to the Idaho Springs area of Colorado to see the glacier. By the time they parked the car and began to hike, it had already become dark. Before they reached the glacier, the two of them turned back. Some other hikers had crossed their path. The hikers told them they still had another half an hour to hike to reach the glacier. Skye and Ensign figured they would cut their losses and not risk hiking in the dark and cold night.

Skye dropped Ensign off at his car. They sat there for a few more minutes as they finished their conversation about armadillos and leprosy in Brazil. They kissed, and Ensign stepped from Skye's car. He needed to find a car of his own, and Skye was set to begin a new job at a veterinary clinic the next morning. Ensign was wearing the Carhart coat...he was prepared for the cold night sitting in his Lexus on the side of the road in Aurora.

Ensign had thousands of contacts in his phone from the years of travel and online interaction. As he sat there, Ensign received a message from Laura. Laura had been following Ensign on the website since early 2018. She lived in Phoenix, Arizona. Laura told Ensign she made arrangements to take a week's vacation the following week. She invited him to stay with her in a hotel in Aurora for her vacation. Ensign accepted the offer. They discussed the details and logistics. With plans set, Ensign got off the phone. He decided to try to get some sleep in the car that night.

The next morning, Unique knocked on Ensign's car door to wake him up. She waited as he gathered up the items he carried with him; mostly drug paraphernalia and small items of value he didn't wish to leave in his car while he was away. Ensign stepped from his car and hopped into the passenger seat of

Unique's Volvo.

"What's the plan?"

"You're going to ride with me to Denver. I need to stop at some stores and then go to the DMV. I have an appointment. I need new tags for my car, since it's almost...MY BIRTHDAY!"

"Well, happy early birthday. Let's roll."

Unique passed him her water pipe. Ensign took a large hit of crystal. As he breathed out a large cloud of smoke, he instantly woke up. The day was ahead of them. Ensign felt good. He pulled out his phone, and he began to search for potential cars on the online market.

After stopping at a few stores, they drove deeper into inner Denver. Eventually, they pulled into a crowded parking lot. Unique left Ensign in the car with her water pipe while she went to handle her business. Ensign watched her walk up to the back of a line of people outside the buildings, across the parking lot. Ensign then scanned the area where Unique was standing.

He saw the situation at the DMV that day; the situation directly resulting from that year's coronavirus pandemic. Disappointment and bad thoughts filled Ensign's head as smoke from the crystal filled Unique's car. The line of people, spaced out at standard increments on the pavement and sidewalk, extended the length of the buildings on the side of the parking lot. The line then turned, and it extended the length of the side of a separate building. Ensign's thoughts began to race.

Unique told Ensign that she had made an appointment. She told him it had been a two-week wait to get the appointment. Ensign saw the line barely moving. He began to think of the complications he was going to face once he actually found a car. He sat in the car for two more hours with the Sun beating down through the car's windows. Unique was a resident of Denver. Unique already had a car. All Unique needed to do was renew her registration. By the time she finally made it back to her car, Ensign had fully exhausted his brain with negative thoughts of the roadblocks he would face when he did manage to procure transportation to leave Colorado.

That Thing at That Place That Time

A car service picked up Ensign from his car on a Friday afternoon. He placed some of his luggage in the trunk. Ensign got in the car and sat down next to Laura. She hugged him, and they kissed. Though they had interacted online for a couple of years, it was the first time Laura and Ensign met in person. As they rode through the city to the other side of Aurora, the two of them talked about how Laura's flight had gone that day. They discussed plans for the upcoming week, and they both agreed they wished to basically remain in the hotel room and order food.

When they reached the hotel, Ensign helped the driver stack Laura's luggage onto a cart outside the hotel lobby. The air in the city was hazy. Not just the air around the hotel. Ensign noticed it the entire drive through the city. The driver left, and Ensign went inside the hotel with Laura.

Ensign waited with the cart as Laura checked into her room at the front desk. She handed him his room key, and the two of them walked to the elevator. Ensign pushed the luggage cart through the lobby and into the elevator. Their room was on the top floor, so Ensign pushed the button to go up.

After he put the luggage on one of the beds, Ensign pushed the empty cart back out into the hallway. Laura undressed him as the door to their room closed behind him. The two of them shared intimacy in the shower. The shower was much needed. It had been a few days since Ensign last showered. Laura put on underwear after they dried off. She requested Ensign remain naked. He obliged.

Laura didn't do drugs. Ensign asked her if she minded if he did. With the confirmation that it was okay with her, Ensign set up his gear on the table by the window. Ensign did a hotrail, and then he also set up his tattoo equipment on the same table. They were many floors up in the hotel. The view overlooking the city to the west was amazing. Ensign sat at the table and did drugs while he tattooed himself.

As the Sun set, the haze in the evening air continued its progression. Laura and Ensign saw three distinct forest fires in the distance. The smoke above the mountains was prominent in the sky. The sunset was beautiful as a result. Ensign had never seen anything like it. From the smoke to the clouds, the sky, and the Sun itself...it was breathtaking. Ensign recorded that first sunset as he did the following sunsets each day from that vantage point high up in their hotel room. The scene was magical and otherworldly. The colors and the sky, the light through the smoke, his mind was blown.

At the end of that week together, Laura gave Ensign an open invitation to come live with her in Phoenix. The offer was appealing, but Ensign's two storage units required his immediate attention. He had to decline Laura's offer. He was sad to part ways with Laura, but the timing hadn't lined up. She went back to Arizona, and Ensign went back to his Lexus on the side of the road in Aurora, Colorado. The air was still hazy, and the fires were still blazing.

Ensign needed a vehicle which had enough space to accommodate the items in his storage unit as well as all the parts he stripped from his Lexus. He found a Subaru Outback on an online car market website which fit that description and was in his price range. Ensign set up a time to meet with the owner for a test drive.

The ride to meet the owner of the Subaru was an expensive trip with a ride service. The drive took forty-five minutes, and the location was in a neighborhood on the far side of Denver. Ensign met the guy at his house, and the ride service drove away. Ensign's wishful thinking was to not need another ride service to return to Aurora. Ensign hoped the car met his expectations, and he would not need any more ride services.

The stars lined up for him that day. The car ran well. The owner and Ensign made a deal. They drove to an ATM so Ensign could take out the remainder of the cash he needed to buy the car. Back at the owner's house, Ensign loaded up four additional tires into the hatchback Subaru. He then had eight tires. He only needed four tires on the car. Ensign took the extra tires anyhow. They went inside, and the owner filled out a bill of sale. He gave Ensign the bill and the title. At that point, Ensign was the owner of the Subaru, title, and all.

Ensign sat down with the previous owner of the Subaru and his wife at their dining room table. They all had celebratory glasses of orange juice to mark the occasion. The Subaru had been the wife's daily driver, but she had upgraded to a newer model. Ensign's story left an impression on the couple. They shared social media information. The couple wished for updates on Ensign's next adventures with the Subaru. When he left, the three of them were all smiling. Ensign hopped in his new car and drove himself back to Aurora.

On his way back to Dean's neighborhood, Ensign stopped at a Walmart. The Subaru was white. Ensign wanted his car to be black. His BMW was black, his Lexus was black, his 3000GT was black and that Subaru needed to fall in line. Ensign bought sandpaper, microfiber rags, clear coat, and black spray paint. He was still working to disassemble his Lexus as much as possible, but he had a new car project. His intake of crystal fueled his motivation.

For the next few days, Ensign alternated between removing components from his Lexus and painting his Subaru. He parked the Subaru directly in front of the Lexus on the street next to Dean's house. Ensign ate meals with Dean and his mother, and he showered at the house. As always, he recorded video to document his activities. As always, he continued his online interactions and dynamics.

As Ensign finished the final coat of black paint on the Subaru, the Sun was almost completely set below the horizon. The neighbor from across the street walked over to talk to him. He extended his hand. They smiled as they shook hands.

"Hi there. I've seen you working hard out here."

As the neighbor and Ensign talked, Ensign told him his story. The neighbor told Ensign a bit about himself. The neighbor then told Ensign a strange story. It caught Ensign's interest instantly. Ensign was both stunned and not surprised at the same time. The neighbor's story was about a lady who walked her dog in the neighborhood. As he told Ensign the story, Ensign realized he hadn't seen the lady walking her dog since close to a week after he had confronted her when she checked the door handle of his car as he was sitting inside.

The neighbor told Ensign how he caught two teenage kids breaking into his car in his driveway. He had them on security camera. The kids had been caught on other security cameras as well; not just in Dean's neighborhood, but in three adjacent neighborhoods. Someone who lived in a neighborhood across the street had also caught the teens in the act. Once police were involved, the teens gave up a lot of information.

It turned out, the lady walking her dog each night was out checking for unlocked car doors. Once it was dark each night, the teens returned to any of the cars which were known to be unlocked. They then stole items from those unlocked cars. The lady walking her dog was the mother of one of those teens.

Ensign shook his head in disbelief as he heard that story. He told the neighbor of his encounter with the lady walking her dog. When their conversation ended, Ensign instantly went into Dean's house to update him on the lady whom he had warned him about previously. Though he knew his encounter with that lady wasn't related to drug paranoia, Ensign was still amazed to hear the way that situation worked out.

Ensign met someone online that night. The guy was a retired lawyer. He lived in Denver. Ensign walked through the neighborhoods to the main shopping strip to meet the guy. When he pulled into the parking lot, Ensign kept his distance. He wasn't sure if it was the lawyer, or not. The SUV was decked out to resemble a police cruiser. Ensign stayed on the edge of the parking lot, out of view until he called the lawyer on the phone. The lawyer confirmed his vehicle was the car in the parking lot which resembled a police car.

Later that night, Shannon instructed Ensign on the videos to make with the lawyer while he was at the lawyer's house. Ensign complied. He showered at the house as the Sun came up the next morning. The lawyer smoked crystal. Ensign's personal supply was dwindling down to nothing, but he still parted with an eightball to increase his funds. When Ensign was dropped back off at his car, he sorted out just how much crystal he had left. Ensign decided he needed one more ounce before he was ready to leave Colorado.

Jump the Shark

That morning, Ensign's task was removing the steering wheel from his Lexus. As he sat in the car, he reached out to Unique. Ensign wasn't able to get in contact with her. He then texted Bethany, his friend from the hotel when he first arrived in Colorado. Though she didn't use crystal, Ensign figured anyone with a black tar heroin connection would most likely be able to score some methamphetamine. Bethany texted Ensign back a moment later. As suspected, she knew a guy.

Bethany named a price for an ounce. It wasn't cheap, but it was still within reason. She told Ensign it would be available at around eight o'clock that night. Ensign thanked her, and he told her he would be in touch. Ensign managed to completely remove his steering wheel. He put it in the hatchback of his Subaru, and he decided he was going to take a shower at Dean's house.

A twenty-five-year-old Puerto Rican girl and Ensign arranged a date at a popular sports bar in Denver that afternoon. After his shower, Ensign drove to Denver to meet up with her. Traffic was terrible. She made it to the bar before he did. There was a festival taking place on the streets outside the sports bar, so Ensign had to park blocks down the street. He was out of breath when he reached the bar.

The girl met him outside. The bar was completely packed; the outside tables and inside of both floors of the establishment were full of bargoers. The two of them walked together through the lower floor of the bar, out to a back patio. They ordered food. The girl ordered a couple drinks. She found it odd that Ensign didn't drink. Their entire interaction from that point was confusing.

The girl was exceptionally beautiful. She told Ensign how attracted to him she was. The vibe was off for Ensign, though. He couldn't figure it out. She seemed half interested in him, but she said random things during their conversation which almost seemed to be insults. When Ensign made jokes, the girl stared blankly at him. She said things which didn't seem to be jokes, and she asked him why he didn't think she was funny.

When the bill came, Ensign reached for it to pay for their meal. The girl took offense and demanded she pay for it. She told Ensign that she would pay, since she was who had invited him on the date. When Ensign tried to retort, the girl genuinely became angry with him. She gave him a ride back to where his car was parked. After she explained how she didn't like his new Subaru, she drove away.

Unique texted Ensign while he was eating his meal at that sports bar. Ensign happened to be on the side of Denver where Unique lived. She told him to stop over. When he got there, Unique introduced Ensign to her brother. The two of them lived together. Unique then motioned him to follow her to the deck in the backyard. As they talked, Unique gave Ensign a price for an ounce. He instantly accepted. Ensign handed her the money from his pocket. She told him she would have the crystal first thing in the morning.

Bethany was unhappy with Ensign when he cancelled his order with her. Ensign told her he couldn't do the price she wanted. Out of courtesy, Ensign told Bethany that if she could match the price that he was getting for it from someone else, then he would still follow through with the deal. Bethany told him she couldn't do it. Ensign told her he was going with his other option. Bethany was mad when she hung up on him. Ensign never meant for her to take it personal. It was business.

The morning later, Ensign was finishing loading his Subaru with Lexus parts. The four extra Subaru tires were jammed into the open space in the empty Lexus. Ensign knew he needed the room in the Subaru for the items in his storage unit. He filled the inside of the Subaru with car stereo equipment, personal belongings, and Lexus parts. Before that though, Ensign blacked out all the back windows with spray paint, left over from painting the car. He didn't want his belongings to be seen through the glass.

Ensign visited the lady working in the office at his storage unit. He closed out his account. He emptied his items from the unit onto a large pushcart. Ensign pushed the cart down the hallways, into the service elevator, and out the front doors to his Subaru. He loaded up his car, and he returned the cart to the lobby of the storage unit. The Subaru was packed as full as his Lexus and BMW had always been as he traveled the country previously, before his plans were put on hold when he broke down in Colorado.

Ensign set a new timeline. He planned to wrap up his affairs and be on the road east within the following five days. With his car loaded completely to the top, Ensign left the storage facility to meet Unique in the parking lot of a strip mall in Denver. Unique had an ounce for him. Ensign needed that crystal to fuel his remaining activities in Aurora, and to then drive across the country once again.

Everything's Always Fine

Ensign called the DMV about an appointment to get license plates for his car. Two weeks. The waiting period for an appointment was two weeks. Ensign knew, from the time he rode with Unique for her appointment, that he wasn't going to be able to get plates for the Subaru. He made up his mind to drive across the country with no license plates on his car. Ensign's time in Colorado had reached expiration.

Ensign worked on the Subaru in the warm Sun. Ensign's Subaru, on the street in Dean's neighborhood, was parked in front of the Lexus. He looked back at his Lexus. Ensign felt a sadness; knowing he was about to leave his car in Colorado. Though he had only owned it since the previous November, he traveled thousands of miles in the Lexus; across most of the country.

While in thought as he stood there, Ensign saw a glint in the sunlight inside the Lexus, below the rearview mirror. He walked over to the Lexus and opened the door. Ensign pulled a knife from his pocket and cut the fishing line from around the mirror. That little metal ninja star was the last item Ensign recovered from his Lexus. It had been hanging from the mirror, as it had in all of his previous cars. Ensign bought the little ninja star from a store in a mall in Toledo, Ohio. He was a teenager when he bought it. It had been with him through his travels. Ensign tied the fishing line around the mirror in his Subaru. He would have forgotten his ninja star had the Sun not shown him the light.

Ensign returned to adjusting the wiring between the Subaru's alternator and battery. He made sure everything was secured and ready to travel. When he was satisfied, he quickly stood up. Ensign forgot that the car's hood was only halfway open. The corner of the hood caught him directly on the top of his head.

Ensign was instantly dazed. He jammed his neck; the hood stopped him from fully standing up. Blood began to stream down Ensign's face and the sides of his head. He felt almost drunk from the head injury. Ensign tried to think, but thoughts weren't coming to him clearly. As blood trailed behind him on the sidewalk, he staggered his way towards Dean's front door. Ensign managed to knock on the front door before he collapsed into a chair on Dean's porch.

Dean's mom opened the door. Through blurred vision, Ensign saw her reaction to his injury. He heard Dean's mom yell for Dean. One of them brought Ensign a bag of ice, and the other brought out paper towels to wrap his head. Ensign wasn't sure who brought what. The bleeding eventually stopped, and Ensign was left with a gash across a swollen knot in the middle of his head. Once he recovered in the chair, Ensign helped Dean wash the blood from the porch. Ensign thanked Dean for the medical treatment.

Ensign then thanked Dean for the hospitality during the entire time he was stranded in Colorado. Ensign let Dean know he would always be genuinely grateful for his help. Dean was a devoted friend to Ensign in a time when he needed one. Ensign knew it was his last twenty-four hours in Colorado.

Ensign spent that night alone. He sat in the Lexus, deep in thought. He hadn't eaten all day. It was eleven o'clock at night when he ordered from a food delivery service. Ensign wanted fried chicken. It was the only thing which sounded good. For the next forty-five minutes, Ensign waited in anticipation.

Ensign's phone vibrated to indicate the delivery driver was approaching. Ensign stepped into the middle of the street for his easy identification. Ensign thanked the driver as he was handed a bag of food...the wrong bag of food. For the next five minutes, Ensign attempted to explain to the driver that he ordered food from a chicken restaurant. Since the driver spoke no English,

Ensign continued to try to hand him back the bag of pancakes from the breakfast diner.

Ensign showed the driver his phone receipt. He showed him the paper receipt taped to the bag. After another minute of attempts to show him the different restaurant logos, the driver reluctantly took the bag back and drove away. Ensign was mad. He instantly contacted customer service. At that point, Ensign was assured the driver would return with the correct order.

Another forty-five minutes slowly ticked by. Again, Ensign waved down the delivery driver as he approached. When the driver handed him the bag of food the second time, Ensign was in disbelief. It contained a burger and French fries from a fast-food restaurant. Ensign made the driver contact his delivery company immediately. They again apologized to Ensign. By then, it was too late. The chicken restaurant was closed.

Ensign took the burger and got on his phone while he ate it in his car. He needed to eat something at that point. Ensign demanded his money back while he unsatisfactorily ate the tiny cold burger. While Ensign angrily sat in his car, a girl pulled up next to him. Ensign stepped out of his car. The girl handed Ensign a bag of fried chicken. Ensign wondered if he was being pranked. He ate the chicken, and he never got an explanation from the delivery company. Ensign did, however, get a refund on his bank card.

The next morning, Ensign took a look around for the last time. He checked throughout the Lexus. He had everything he needed and wanted to bring with him. He started the Subaru, and he pulled from Dean's neighborhood. Ensign's mind was heavy with thoughts...and saturated with drugs. He felt free, he felt excited, and he felt empty inside.

When Ensign reached the eastern outskirts of the Denver metro area, a weird feeling came over him. He was leaving. He stopped at a gas station. He sent a few text messages while he was inside the store. After he paid for his gas, Ensign walked outside and filled up his tank. He looked around one last time. Ensign got in his car, and he left Colorado.

Ways Did

Shannon decided which route Ensign took east across the country. Ensign told Shannon he could take Interstate 80 or Interstate 70. I-80 would take him across the country more to the north, through Omaha, Des Moine, and Chicago. I-70 would take him a more southern route, through Kansas City, St. Louis, and Indianapolis. Ensign asked Shannon which route to take. Shannon told him to take Interstate 70.

Ensign decided to pass over the border to Kansas before he stopped for sleep that first night of the trip. The Subaru held up well. At a rest stop in Kansas, Ensign shut his eyes. Colorado was behind him. He was sad to leave, but he was excited for the next chapter. Ensign had drugs, and he hopefully had enough money for gasoline and food the rest of the trip.

Ensign woke up with the rising Sun...because the heat and bright light were unbearable; directly on him, the sunlight shone through his car's closed windows. Ensign realized, in that uncomfortable moment, that he needed to prioritize acquiring and fitting new window shades for the Subaru.

The cross-country drive back to the Midwest was mostly uneventful. Ensign didn't have license plates, so he inevitably encountered law enforcement. The first instance occurred at a gas station in Topeka, Kansas. The officer walked up to Ensign's car as he sat in a parking space, eating a slice of pizza. Ensign explained his story; why he didn't have plates on the car. He told the officer about finally leaving Colorado after months of being stranded on the road in Aurora. He told him about the wait for an appointment at the DMV. Ensign told him about his storage unit in Ohio.

The crystal had Ensign talking more than the officer cared to listen. The officer let him go, but Ensign asked him one question as the officer turned to walk away. The question was answered in detail. Ensign appreciated his response, and he let the officer get back to his business. Thanks to the officer's answer, Ensign then had directions to the best fried chicken in the Topeka area.

Days later, Ensign reached Illinois. He saw the police cruisers positioned in the median of the highway to catch speeders. Traffic was the heaviest he had seen it during the pandemic times. He drove past the cruisers with cars in the lanes beside him. He drove past the cruisers with cars in the lanes in front of him and behind him. Three minutes later, Ensign saw the blue and red lights behind him.

Ensign pulled over to the side of the road, and the officer approached his car. Again, the crystal had Ensign talking. As soon as Ensign rolled down his window, he jumped right into his story. The officer looked at Ensign; wide-eyed as he took in sentence after sentence of dialogue. He told the officer about months spent in Aurora, the wait for an appointment at the DMV, and his storage unit back in Perrysburg. Ensign told him about his last interaction with the police and the fried chicken.

When the officer finally managed to speak a sentence of his own, he told Ensign to hang on for a minute while he walked back to his car. Ensign looked around to make sure all his drugs were put away. His car was packed with his belongings. The only available open space was where he sat in the driver's seat. Ensign's drugs and paraphernalia were stashed amongst the clutter. He wasn't sure exactly where all of his illegal items were at, but nothing was in plain sight.

Five minutes later, the officer was back at Ensign's window. Ensign's license came back clean. The officer handed Ensign a paper. He told Ensign to keep it in case he was pulled over again on his drive. He told Ensign it would save time. It was a note which explained he was going to get plates once he was back in Ohio. The officer quickly bid Ensign a safe trip and sent him on his way before Ensign could again bombard him with incessant talking.

Ensign woke up the next morning at another rest stop. He was still in Illinois. Ensign replied to a message on his phone. After he blew down a couple hotrails, he got on the road again. Ensign had the directions in his phone. He needed to shower, and a girl from an app had offered for him to use her shower. She wanted to watch. Ensign accepted the offer to shower and eat lunch at his new friend's apartment.

Isochrone Curve

It was the day before Halloween in 2020. Though his drug supply was still topped off, Ensign's money supply had trickled down to almost nonexistent. He was on the final stretch of his cross-country drive. Ensign checked his phone. He had sixty dollars in his bank account and no cash in his wallet. He had enough money to fuel up the Subaru one more time. Ensign was an hour and a half from his destination in Ohio when his gas gauge went into the red.

Ensign pulled into a travel center from the highway in Indiana. He parked at a gas pump and walked into the store to prepay. Ensign wore the Carhart coat which Skye had given him. It was cold. He felt the Midwest winter moving in. It was late in the night, but Ensign was determined to make it to his destination without any more stops after that travel center. He had slept in his car for too long. Ensign wanted to sleep inside a house. Ensign updated Adrian on his location, and he gave Adrian an estimated time for his arrival in Findlay, Ohio early that next morning.

Ensign scrunched up his face as he read the screen on the machine. He tried again…and a third time. The card reader at the check-out counter declined his bank card. Ensign stepped out of line and checked his account on his phone. He had sixty dollars. He showed his phone screen to the cashier. Ensign got back in line. He tried his card again.

"The transaction cannot be completed."

Ensign called the customer service phone number for his

bank. He reached an automated recording. It was far outside of normal business hours. He was prompted to try again when the bank opened on the next business day. Ensign's chemically saturated mind raced to thoughts of bad situations and doom. He was so close, yet he may as well have been a million miles away without gasoline in his car. He didn't even have enough gas to make it to another gas station to try a different card reader.

During his tenure in Lansing, Michigan in the spring of 2020, Ensign made many friends. One friend from Lansing had an interesting name. His name was Pure Energy. Ensign first met Pure Energy at Simon and Caleb's apartment, and the two of them grew close during the time Ensign spent in the area. Pure Energy and Ensign stayed in touch as Ensign traveled the country. The two of them remained in contact on Ensign's drive back to the Midwest.

Ensign sent Pure Energy a text from the gas station in Indiana. Ensign hadn't asked him for money, but Pure Energy sent Ensign fifty dollars as soon as Ensign told Pure Energy he was stranded. Ensign filled his gas tank, relieved to have hurdled that final obstacle which almost kept him from reaching his goal.

Ensign reached that goal early that Halloween morning. He stood in the darkness and knocked on Adrian's door. A moment later, the porch light turned on and the front door opened. Ensign greeted Adrian and walked inside to the living room. He put his bags down next to the couch, and he fell fast asleep moments after lying down on that couch. Ensign managed a few hours of non-car sleep for the first time in a while.

Ensign did some hotrails with Adrian and his boyfriend when he woke up later that morning. After they ate breakfast, he gathered up his belongings. Ensign let Adrian know he would be back in the evening. He had a full day's worth of work to do at his storage unit. He had items to unload from his Subaru, he had a completely full storage unit to sort through, and he had to select the new priority items to load back into his car for travel.

Ensign needed to pick out which items from his car and

from storage he was going to try to sell. His y-pipe exhaust system, which Dan had never managed to replace on his Lexus, was going to be an item he tried to sell. Ensign's custom Lexus bumper, which was put on his Lexus just prior to leaving to head west, was also going to go up for sale. Ensign had removed it from the Lexus in Colorado. It barely fit in his Subaru. Those two items were extremely space consuming, so Ensign prioritized selling them first. Ensign already had a party interested in the bumper.

Methamphetamine got the best of him while at his storage unit. Hours were spent rummaging, sorting, and moving items all over the unit and the pavement outside it. Ensign came across a can of gold spray paint, left over from painting the emblem of the Lexus bumper months before. The crystal put an idea in his head. An hour later, Ensign's Subaru, formerly white and then all black, had gold tiger stripes all over it.

Ideas inspired by crystal meth are seldom thought through to logical conclusion. The y-pipe Lexus exhaust system was easily seven feet long from end to end. On one side, there was a single metal tube resembling a bazooka. On the other side, the two pipes with catalytic converters curved outward from the center of the assembly. It looked like a giant metal "y," hence the term "y-pipe."

Ensign had another crystal idea, and he put it into crystal action. He strapped the y-pipe to the roof rack of the Subaru. The front bazooka end extended forward above the middle of his car's windshield. The two rear metal tubes sat above either side of the roof rack extending to the back of the Subaru's roof. It literally looked like a military weapon on the top of the car... especially once the crystal convinced him it was a good idea to spray paint the y-pipe gold to match the tiger stripes all over the car. Ensign had created a rolling, driving eyesore.

The modifications to the tiger striped doom bringer were set. Ensign unloaded much of his haul from the other side of the country. He picked up new items from his storage unit to aid in his future travels. He made a stop at a rest stop on his meandering route from Perrysburg back to Adrian's house in Findlay. The crystal in Ensign's brain managed to send him about an hour out of the way west from Adrian's house. Crystal seemed to lead Ensign to seek out rest stops anywhere he went. If there were no rest stops on Ensign's immediate route, crystal encouraged him to divert until he came across one...even when his destination was closer than the rest stop.

Ensign parked the doom bringer, and he walked to the restroom in the main building at the rest stop. When he got back to his car, he realized he locked his keys inside his ridiculous looking vehicle. It was sunset, and the air was cold. Ensign shook his head, and he got to work. So many times, his cars had been unlocked by prying open and wedging the corner of a window. Ensign needed some sticks and a rock.

Ensign looked around until he found what he thought would work. It didn't work. For six hours, it didn't work. His phone was locked in his car. He had nobody to call. It grew dark outside. Ensign walked a substantial distance to the opposite side of the rest stop where there was semi parking. Ensign figured he could find someone with tools to help. The first truck, Ensign knocked with no answer. The second truck's driver was sitting in the front seat. As Ensign approached, before he even spoke, the truck driver yelled, "No!" and rolled up his window.

When Ensign got back to his car, he abandoned the effort on his driver's side window. Crystal told him the passenger side had a better chance of success. Another hour went by. It was windy and snowing. A car of four people in their early twenties pulled into a parking space a couple of spaces down from Ensign. Three of them went into the building with the restrooms. The fourth walked over to Ensign.

"What do you have going on over here?"

The guy tried to help Ensign while his friends were inside the building. The other three tried to join in the effort once they returned to the parking lot. Nothing worked. Ensign thanked them, and he told them he would manage somehow. They left and got back onto the highway. Two minutes later, Ensign almost had the window pried open enough to reach in with a stick and unlock the door...and then the entire passenger side window shattered.

Glass exploded into the car and all over the parking space next to the Subaru. Ensign pulled a battery powered vacuum cleaner from the back of the car and sucked up all the glass from the front seat and the pavement. He unloaded the new window shades he made. He duct taped the layers of shades to the inside and outside of the broken window.

Ensign dreaded the drive back to Adrian's house on that cold pre-winter night. He knew he needed to get to a hardware store the next day for caulk and a thick sheet of Plexi glass. The tiger striped doom machine was downgraded another notch that night at the rest stop. Ensign's modifications to his Subaru were a physical manifestation of the modifications which crystal was doing to his brain.

Canon Foder

In Colorado, Ensign dropped his phone on Dean's patio in the back yard. Dropping the phone set a timer on the phone. Ensign bought that phone in spring, before he left the Midwest. The timer detonated as he sat on the couch in Adrian's living room. The screen went black, and bright light came from the cracks. One minute, Ensign was sending messages. The next minute, all the information in that phone was lost forever. Ten thousand videos and pictures from 2020 were no longer accessible. Texts and messages disappeared instantly. Ensign pulled out an old phone and picked up where he left off.

It was cold outside, but Adrian had the heat turned up high in his house. Ensign sat on the couch in boxer shorts. Suddenly, he was hungry. He had his long black trench coat with him. Ensign decided it was easier to throw that on and go get food from a gas station without getting dressed.

At first glance, Ensign looked like a stereotypical flasher. His chest and legs were bare. He looked unclothed underneath the trench coat. It was late, and he didn't care. Ensign assumed he wouldn't see anyone but the gas station clerk that late in Findlay, Ohio. That small farm town was empty at peak hours, and it was one o'clock in the morning.

When he reached the gas station five minutes up the road, Ensign saw three guys in their twenties standing outside the entrance. Ensign parked at a gas pump since he needed gas anyhow. The three guys stared at him from across the parking lot. They saw Ensign step from a ridiculous car wearing what looked to be only a trench coat. They quickly seemed to lose interest. One of the guys ran around the side of the building while the other two walked into the store ahead of him.

As Ensign grabbed a drink and a carton of eggs from the refrigerator at the back of the store, he heard the two guys talking loudly with the cashier. Ensign walked across the store and over to the counter to pay for his items and prepay for gasoline. The two guys were in front of him in line. One continued to converse with the cashier, but the other turned to Ensign and stared. Ensign nodded to him. The guy then began to speak.

"Uh, what are you doing?"

"I'm buying eggs and a Yoo-Hoo."

"Uh, why?"

"Because I want eggs and a Yoo-Hoo."

The guy continued to stare at him, indignant. Ensign stared back. The guy finally broke his gaze when the cashier, whom Ensign assumed was one of his friends, told the two guys to step aside so he could ring Ensign up. The two guys walked out of the store, and Ensign paid for his items. He asked the cashier a question.

"What was that all about?"

"Don't mind them. They're idiots."

Ensign stepped out into the night with his eggs and Yoo-Hoo and began to cross the parking lot to go pump his gas. Suddenly, he saw movement to his right side, on the other side of the lot. From over the hill, between the gas station and the business next door, the two guys reappeared. With them was the guy seen earlier running behind the building when Ensign pulled up. There was also a fourth guy Ensign hadn't seen before. They were in a hurry, heading directly for him. Ensign was halfway between the store and his car, alone in the night.

Ensign waited to be sure they were intent on him. They were. The guy who spoke to Ensign in the store had a huge smile on his face. Ensign let them get closer. He stopped in the open parking lot between the store entrance and the gas pumps. He stared at them. They looked like they were closing in on their prey. Their prey, on that night, was Ensign.

Ensign let them reach the edge of the row of gas pumps. He calmly reached his hand into the right-side pocket of his trench coat. Surprise. Ensign pulled out his nine-millimeter handgun. All four sets of eyes instantly widened. Ensign kept the gun pointed down, but he reached over with his left hand and racked the slide.

All four surprised guys instantly scattered. The guy who previously ran behind the building again ran behind the building. The other three, no longer frozen in their tracks, turned tail and booked it back up and over the hill to the building next door. Ensign stood there for another thirty seconds. He unracked his gun and casually walked to his car and pumped thirty dollars of prepaid gas.

Ensign didn't know those guys' intentions that night, but he never had to find out. There were no injuries on either side in that battle. That battle was stopped before it became a thing. Ensign's gun saved at least three people from being hurt that night. Ensign would have been one of the victims of violence, but he was sure he would have at least managed to inflict damage to two of the four of them, if not more. Instead, nobody was hurt...except maybe some egos.

All the situations and predicaments he'd faced in seedy areas and large cities, doing questionable things with questionable people, and it was four farm boys in a tiny Ohio town who forced Ensign's hand as close as he had ever been to pulling the trigger. He was beside himself as he drove back to Adrian's house, if for nothing but that fact alone. Ensign told Adrian and his boyfriend the story of four lucky trash balls and cool heads prevailing that night.

Game On

Ensign originally left Michigan in spring of 2020 to start over. He left the Midwest to get out of the game. The game pulled him back in. Ensign didn't know what else to do. He chose the route which had been good to him. Despite the stress and the complications, Ensign knew he was able to get ahead again with the business model he followed for the past few years. In his mind, his chemically filled mind, it was an easy choice to make.

Back at Adrian's house, Ensign started making phone calls. The first call he made was to set up a junkyard in Colorado to come pick up his Lexus from the side of the road. Out of courtesy, Ensign told Dean he would have his Lexus removed from the street beside Dean's house. The junkyard offered him three hundred and fifty dollars for scrapping his car. They insisted Ensign didn't need to be there for them to tow it and pay him. They told him a tow truck would be there in three days to pick it up.

Ensign got in contact with a guy interested in buying his Lexus bumper. The two of them set up a plan; Ensign would drop the bumper off at a shipping company, and the guy would then send Ensign half of the money upon the shipping receipt. Once the bumper arrived in Texas, he would send Ensign the other half of the agreed price. The guy would pay the shipping costs.

Ensign's next phone calls became a sort of grassroots fundraiser for illicit substances. Ensign wanted to take a ride. He wanted to pick up supplies. He wanted to jump right back in the game, right where he left off in spring before leaving the Midwest. Ensign was trustworthy, and his friends and associates knew it. Close to a thousand dollars was sent to Ensign to jumpstart his efforts.

Ensign made a phone call to someone he hadn't spoken with since spring of that year. Ensign told his plug that he wanted an amount beyond what he could cover at the moment. Ensign knew more people were in the process of freeing up funds to front him. Ensign told his plug that he would see him in a few hours. Ensign had to drive to him, and he was planning to drop off the bumper along the way.

Ensign did just that. He dropped off the bumper at a courier service along the way. The guy in Texas sent Ensign the first half of that money and the shipping cost. Ensign switched gears as he left the courier. He texted his plug, and he added on to his order.

Ensign stopped at a rest stop a bit later. Two other friends sent him money. Ensign sent them messages confirming he would see them once he made it back from the spot. Ensign texted his plug again and added to the order another time. Trust goes a long way in life. Money came in because Ensign's friends in the game knew he was good on his word. Ensign reached his destination, having added on to the order yet one more time along the way. Just like that, Ensign was back in the game.

Those next couple days were spent driving here and there, dropping off items and recouping the funds Ensign lost during his time across the country. Ensign also received a message and money from the guy in Texas when he confirmed the arrival of the Lexus bumper.

Ensign heard back from the junkyard in Colorado. The tow truck driver called him as he was on the street next to Dean's house. Though Ensign mentioned to the tow truck driver that he was told he didn't need to be present for them to tow his car, the driver told Ensign he had been misinformed. There was nothing Ensign could do about that. He was not going back to Colorado. Ensign accepted that he was not going to get paid to scrap his Lexus.

Dean told Ensign the city came out and towed the Lexus a

week later. Ensign let go of that situation once he confirmed his car was no longer sitting on the street by Dean's house. That officially closed the chapter of Ensign's life with his Lexus. He was happy the car was handled so Dean didn't have to think about it or see it anymore.

It was early November of 2020. Ensign thought he could make a clean break from the lifestyle he had been living up until spring of that year. He managed to leave Lansing, Michigan in the past, but he was right back doing what he had been doing to make money. It was game on.

Ensign was online interacting the same as he had been. He was receiving payments from the website. He was meeting old and new people from the internet for intimate connections. Ensign was doing drugs at the exact same high rate daily, and he was traveling all over the place. Without Lansing as his home base, Ensign was more homeless than ever.

Ensign left Adrian's house. He headed to Chicago. He planned to meet up with someone he met on the internet. They were going to spend a weekend together, and then Ensign was going to head to a spot outside Ann Arbor, Michigan. Ensign had found somewhere to stay in Michigan while he put a plan of action together.

In Chicago, Ensign met with the internet hookup outside of the hotel where they planned to stay for two nights. The lady was a pretty Black girl. She was thirty-five years old. After meeting up, she went in and checked into the room. She gave Ensign the second key card when she came back out to the parking lot. They each got in their cars and drove around to the other side of the building, closer to their hotel room.

Ensign indulged in the woman's fantasies during their time together. After the weekend, Ensign was sore from her activity. Ensign enjoyed the intimacy, but he felt relief when he left Chicago. The two of them became close during the weekend, but they went their separate ways on the Monday morning after their time together.

Ensign texted Karen as he left Chicago. He let her know he was on his way. He then typed in her address in Ann Arbor, Michigan and settled in for the drug-fueled hours of driving ahead of him. Karen was a former scientist with a PhD. She was highly intelligent. She finished school early after skipping a few grades when she was young. Ensign first met Karen on the website in 2019. She was a year older than him, and she lived alone in a quiet neighborhood outside Ann Arbor.

Though Karen was married, her husband lived in North Carolina, working his job as an environmental engineer. The couple had been separated since before Ensign first met Karen the prior year. Karen no longer worked as a scientist. She remained at home most of the time to focus on her mental health. Though Ensign had never met Karen's husband, Karen assured Ensign he was good to come stay with her in his absence.

Ensign hadn't slept for days. He hadn't slept since mid-week before he went to Chicago. He did drugs to try to keep his eyes open as he drove. Ensign knew he was pushing his limit and needed to sleep. He was determined to reach Karen's house without pulling over somewhere to sleep. Hours later, Ensign made it to Ann Arbor, Michigan. He was on the home stretch, and he felt relieved when he pulled his ridiculous car into Karen's driveway.

Burnin' Down the House

Ensign was happy to see Karen. His mind was compromised from the lack of sleep. Ensign set up the hotrail tray and blew down some lines with Karen. He was so tired. He was exhausted mentally and physically. Shortly after he sat down on the big black leather reclining couch in the living room, Ensign fell out. He didn't just fall asleep; he almost instantly went into a comatose level of unconsciousness as his mind and body gave out on him completely.

Ensign remembered waking up just one time during the many hours he was unconscious. He didn't know where he was. He didn't recognize anything. He seemed to be in a house, but he didn't know whose house. In a trance-like state, Ensign remembered stumbling down a hallway to look for a bathroom. He had to pee.

As he made his way back to the living room, Ensign stumbled past a woman he didn't recognize. He remembered the look on her face. She looked angry. Neither of them said a word as they passed by each other. Ensign heard a door in the hallway close behind him. He fell asleep as he slumped down to the floor in the living room. He didn't even make it back to a couch.

Ensign could tell much more time had passed when he again regained semi-consciousness. He was awake, but he remained lying there on the floor in the same position with his eyes closed. Ensign heard talking. It was a woman's voice. He listened for who else was involved in the conversation. There was only one voice. The conversation was one woman speaking to herself.

Ensign was still tired and had no desire to open his eyes. He rolled over at one point and opened his eyes for a second. Ensign focused on a couch in his line of sight. Personal belongings were stacked around Karen, where she sat talking to herself. She hadn't seen Ensign was awake, and he closed his eyes again. A moment later, as a result of what he heard Karen say, his eyes instantly opened wide. Ensign jumped up from the floor.

"Karen, hi. I'm sorry I slept for so long. I hadn't slept in days."

Karen stared at Ensign. She had a concerning look on her face as she mumbled to herself.

"Karen! Snap out of it."

Karen instantly looked shocked. She stared at Ensign in disbelief. Then, she spoke to him.

"You can see me? You can see me here in front of you?"

"Of course I can see you. I'm sorry I slept so long. I needed the sleep. Don't do it. I see you. You exist, I promise you."

A moment prior, Ensign had suddenly jumped up from where he had been on the floor in response to Karen's conversation with herself. Karen was convinced she was a ghost. She was going to burn the house down with them in it to prove she no longer existed. Ensign jumped up to reply to her just in time. All the items stacked on the couch around Karen were items from her life which were important to her. Until Ensign jumped up from the floor, she was convinced she had to start the fire.

Karen told Ensign that while she was awake tweaking by herself, she had spent hours shaking him and yelling to him, trying to wake him up. Her mind concluded Ensign was dead. Since he hadn't recognized or acknowledged her earlier when he walked in a haze to find a bathroom, Karen took it as he was unable to see her...because she had become a ghost. Ensign was relieved he woke up when he had. He was relieved he paid attention to her conversation with herself as he was lying on the floor. He was relieved he managed to convince her she was a real person, and they both, for sure, were very much alive.

Ensign was no longer tired. He set up his hotrail tray, and he began his day in typical fashion; by blowing down a few large lines of crystal.

Ensign told Karen his plan for his time at her house: he was going to order parts and audio equipment online, and along with multiple trips to local stores for supplies, he was going to turn his Subaru into a camper/stereo on wheels. Ensign was going to stay in the game for the immediate future. He was going to cash in on the website and get a substantial paycheck from his online popularity. After that, he was going to get his registration and plates for the car. It was also the year Ensign needed to renew his driver's license. When all of that was done, Ensign was planning to head down to Florida, away from the cold of winter...and closer to Shannon.

With respect to the game, Ensign agreed to make a trip up to Lansing, Michigan. Though he vowed to avoid Lansing at all costs, he convinced himself that the potential money was worth a quick in-and-out. Ensign went to Brittany's house by himself one evening. He took Karen's car, since his car was in her garage in the process of being worked on. A couple of other people Ensign knew from Lansing were over at Brittany's house when he arrived. He made sure he was in and out within an hour. Ensign stopped at a rest stop on the way back, and he checked the outside and thoroughly underneath the car for anything out of place or suspicious. When he was sure the car was clean, Ensign drove back to Karen's house.

Ensign was down by Dayton, Ohio one afternoon, and he stopped at a chili dog restaurant to eat. As he sat in the parking lot, he saw police cruisers with flashing lights drive by him on the highway he was facing...then he saw more...and then more. He began to record video. For a half hour, dozens and dozens of police cars raced by him. He had to look up what was happening. It turned out, there was an active shooter at the outdoor swap meet a quarter mile down the road.

While down in the Dayton area, Ensign met with his friend Felicity at a hotel for the afternoon. They had been talking, and they both wished to experience something together. A recent mother, Felicity had her mom and stepdad babysit her kid for the afternoon. A recent mother, Felicity breastfed Ensign in the hotel room. It was intimate. It was a close and beautiful way for them to bond as they shared that time and activity. He treasured the connection and their activity together.

Ensign spent hours in the large, attached garage of Karen's house working on his car. Multiple days would pass without Ensign knowing if and when it was daytime or nighttime. Drugs were constantly being consumed. Periodically, Ensign would go into the house and walk to the other side and deliver drugs to Karen in her bedroom. Sometimes, they didn't see each other for days.

One day, Ensign attempted to organize the videos he had created. Ensign plugged his backup drive into his laptop as he sat in the Subaru in the garage. Drugs, barely any food, and a full week later, Ensign abandoned the task for the time being. He made a tiny amount of progress, but the well-over hundred thousand media items Ensign previously created were still nowhere near organized and categorized on his storage drive. Ensign created two terabits of media. The task of organization overwhelmed him. Ensign put the laptop aside and got back to the work on his car.

Another amplifier and a ten-inch subwoofer delivered to Karen's house. Ensign added them to the other amplifiers and speakers in the car. He used spray foam, wood, paint, and other supplies to totally redo the inside and outside of the car. Ensign had his tools with him, and Karen's garage was full of power tools.

At one point, early on as Ensign was staying with Karen, he

was on the way home from his storage unit in Perrysburg. A fire started behind the dashboard. When he made it back to Karen's house, Ensign spent the next week removing all the wires in the entire car. He then replaced any damaged wires and re-installed the entire car's wiring. Methamphetamine fueled his obsessive car work. Karen was out of town that week, and Ensign filled her entire living room with the wiring he was repairing and replacing. He finished the project the day before Karen came back home.

Ensign stopped to see his friend Steve in Tecumseh. Steve had to go to work, but he gave Ensign his bank card to take to the ATM and withdrawal the money to pay him for some supplies. Ensign hadn't seen Steve in a while, but he used to handle business with Steve frequently in that way. Another benefit of being trustworthy.

Ensign's friend Betsy was still avoiding crack and sticking with crystal. Ensign was with Betsy one day at a friend of hers in Michigan who happened to own a bunch of property. After they engaged in sexual activity in a barn in the backyard, the two of them wandered around in the woods out back of the house. They came upon a small wooden shack. Inside was all the equipment of an old, abandoned meth lab. Surprisingly, it was the first and only meth lab Ensign had ever seen. Betsy and Ensign engaged in sexual activity in the meth lab.

Ensign was working towards being able to head to Florida, but he encountered a snag. He received notification from the website that his payment was delayed. Ensign had to let Karen know he was going to be there a bit longer until the payment came through. He needed the money. Ensign made money in the game during that time, but he wanted that payment from the website for funding to travel across the country again. Karen understood, and it wasn't an issue.

Ensign read something one day on an online forum. It was a

post about taking antacids and then eating a shard of crystal. He did some research and learned what he wanted to learn. Ensign then tried it himself. Though he had always been able to handle his crystal, Ensign finally felt what it must be like for those zombie tweakers he had seen in videos. It overwhelmed his mind and body. He didn't like the experience at all, and he held out in the garage for hours before he came down enough not to feel completely wasted. Ensign vowed to never do that again.

Ensign didn't pry into Karen's business, so he didn't know her situation with her separated husband. One afternoon, there was a knock on the door. Ensign looked through the peep hole. He instantly walked back to Kate's bedroom and knocked on her door. It was law enforcement. He stood in the living room as Karen answered the door. It was a welfare check. Karen's husband had called the police when he couldn't reach Karen on the phone that day. The officer left soon after arriving, but Karen mentioned it happened frequently.

Ensign met his friend Meg on the website during another week when Karen was out of town. Meg also used crystal, and she had her own supply. She came over to Karen's house one night to hang out. Ensign tattooed her side by her stomach. They kissed, but they didn't have sex. Ensign instantly liked Meg. They got along well. They began to hang out on a regular basis.

Tomato Can Resilience

Karen was also out of town for the week of Thanksgiving. She traveled far up North to spend the holiday with her family in upper Michigan. Ensign met a trans girl on an app a couple of days after Thanksgiving. Though Karen had her car with her, Ensign chose to do what he had been doing anytime he needed to use his car for travel. He put it back together enough to make it drivable, and he drove it. Ensign drove his car to St. Clair Shores, Michigan to meet Sophie two days after they first came into contact online.

Sophie was a pretty girl in her early twenties. She lived in the top part of her dad's house in a neighborhood in St Clair Shores. Sophie and Ensign spent the evening doing drugs and making intimate videos together. Yet again, Ensign was at a point where he hadn't slept in a few days. He managed to stay up for a few hours, but he eventually passed out.

Ensign had a weird dream where he was standing in Sophie's bathroom trying to pee. Each time he tried to use the bathroom, he couldn't because two unidentifiable people behind him were jamming the end of a Christmas tree up his butt. Ensign abruptly woke up from the dream. He was confused, until he realized why he had been having that dream.

Ensign woke up on his stomach. His boxer shorts were down around his legs. Sophie was on top of him and inside of him, thrusting away. Ensign let her go for a few more minutes, but eventually his urge to pee had him have her stop. The two of them hadn't had intercourse up until that point, and he had not previously agreed to it.

Ensign tattooed himself some more that morning at Sophie's house. He also tattooed two small purple hearts on Sophie's cheekbones below her eyes. They each did more drugs, and Ensign left St. Clair to head back to Ann Arbor to work more on his car.

Karen arrived back home a few days later. Ensign continued to travel the tri-state area and make money. Ensign took Karen's car most of the time. Karen also gave him her car to take on trips to re-up. Unless Karen traveled out of town, she spent her time in her bedroom.

Ensign finished the structural work on his Subaru. He finished the wiring and the audio system. He painted the outside once more, light green with black accents and a white roof. It looked ridiculous again, but Ensign's crystal-soaked brain was happy...for the moment. Suddenly, Ensign decided he needed to paint his car again. He went out and bought more spray paint. He then painted his Subaru one more time. He painted it completely black, same as it was before.

Back when Ensign was thirty years old and in college for psychology in Toledo, he befriended a beautiful girl named Amy. Ensign was in an unhealthy relationship at the time, and he was addicted to heroin before he had back surgery. Amy was his age, and she was a former exotic dancer. The two of them met in a shared government class in college. Amy and Ensign never were sexual back when he was thirty, but there was an undeniable attraction...at least on his end.

The two of them hung out while at school and a few times out of class. They did some drugs together, but they were both in relationships at the time, so it never turned sexual. Later on, they reconnected when Ensign worked for a company in Dundee, Michigan. Amy lived in a small city fifteen minutes north. Again, they lost contact...until Ensign came across her profile on a social media site one day while working on his car in Karen's garage.

Karen didn't need her car for the next few days, so Ensign drove it over to Amy's house. Amy still lived in the same house she had when Ensign worked in Dundee. Their connection picked up right where it had left off. They played house for the next two days. They made love and shared intimacy. They laughed, they cried, they connected. Ensign then needed to get Karen's car back to her. The two of them parted ways with a "to be continued" vibe...though Ensign wasn't ever able to continue that journey with Amy.

A day later, Ensign received the check from the website. He finalized his plans to leave the Midwest once again. By the beginning of the next week, Ensign was going to be back on the road. One more week in the cold Michigan weather. Ensign was then going to head down to warm Florida and better times. He was again excited to escape the Midwest. Ensign had tried earlier in the year, and after being stranded in Colorado, he was back in Michigan. It was time for redemption.

Ride The Wave

Karen had been busy behind the closed door of her bedroom. She had procured an online, long-distance boyfriend. Her boyfriend coincidentally lived in North Carolina, the same state as her husband. Though Karen's new boyfriend, Tom, was on parole for something in North Carolina, he showed up at the house in Michigan, invited by Karen. Tom was a decent enough guy, and Ensign had one more client before he left for Florida.

Ensign mostly stayed in his camper-car in the garage. Karen and Tom stayed on the opposite side of the house in Karen's bedroom. Ensign walked from the garage into the house one morning after he returned with Karen's car from a trip to reup. Karen and Tom had been waiting on him.

Ensign took off his long sleeve shirt and hung it over the back of a chair in the dining room. He sat down at the head of the dining room table and unzipped his backpack. Ensign took out a couple of handfuls of bags from inside the backpack. Ensign repeated the process a couple times. A moment later, he had lined up the sixteen bags on the table, each containing an ounce of large, high-grade crystals. Ensign pulled out a digital scale, and he began to weigh out eightballs from one of the bags. Karen paid him prior to taking the trip, so Ensign tossed an eightball to Karen and another eightball to Tom.

As the two of them pocketed the bags, Ensign continued to weigh out the contents from the bag he had used to supply them. There was a knock on the door. Ensign froze. Before Karen even made it to the front door, Ensign heard a key unlock the door. A police officer stepped into the house and Karen's husband barged in past him.

Karen's husband found out previously that Karen had a boyfriend. He learned from Karen's family that her boyfriend skipped out on his parole and was visiting Karen in Michigan. Karen's husband came back to his Michigan house from North Carolina when he heard the news, and he brought the police with him to arrest Tom.

At the moment Ensign froze, Tom ran through the kitchen into the garage to hide. Ensign stood up in front of the dining room table. As the officer, Karen's husband, and another officer entered the front room of the house, Ensign thought of options as fast as he could. Ensign had a pound of crystal laid out on the dining room table. Before any of the visitors looked in his direction, Ensign quickly took his shirt from the back of the chair and threw it over the top of the dining room table. He then walked to the living room to keep any attention away from the dining room table.

Karen's husband yelled at Karen the entire time he was in the house. The officers attempted to calm him down multiple times. Karen's husband looked at Ensign. Ensign wasn't who he was looking for. He turned to Karen.

"Where is he?!"

Tom came back inside from the garage. Karen's husband saw Tom as he walked into the living room to stand next to Karen. Karen's husband ran up to Tom and got directly in his face.

"That's him! It's him right here! Arrest him!"

One of the officers told the husband he needed to step outside with him to calm down. The other officer remained in the living room, close to the front door. Ensign slunk his way back to he dining room table. Ensign was in direct view of the officer, t the officer was occupied speaking with Karen and Tom. en's husband was outside, yelling incessantly. Ensign saw gh the window that at least one more officer had joined the commotion outside.

In the moments when the officer inside was distracted and focused away from Ensign, Ensign began to scoop up his shirt on the table with the bags of drugs underneath. The moment came when Ensign was sure he could scoop up all from underneath the shirt into his arms with the shirt. Ensign casually picked up his belongings and walked from the dining room as nonchalantly as he could.

He walked through the kitchen, still in view of the others. Once Ensign made it to the hallway leading to the garage, he balled up his shirt in his hands to be sure he didn't drop anything. In the garage, Ensign stashed his shirt and its contents under the bed in his camper-car. His hands were shaking from adrenaline. Ensign stayed in the garage, but he locked his car and worked on a project on the other side of the garage.

Eventually, Ensign heard the door shut. Everyone had left the house except Karen and Tom. Ensign walked back into the living room. The three of them were in shock. The police hadn't been in contact with authorities in North Carolina, so they had no cause to take Tom with them. All they had was the word of Karen's irate husband. Tom dodged a bullet that day...Ensign dodged a nuclear bomb.

Ensign texted Meg. Meg lived an hour west of Ann Arbor. After that incident, Ensign felt he needed to be at least that far away from Ann Arbor. He packed up all his belongings. Ensign already had almost everything loaded in his car in preparation to head to Florida. Within an hour, Ensign left in his camper-car to spend the night at Meg's house.

The next morning at Meg's house, Ensign realized he had a couple more items still at Karen's house which he wanted to take with him to Florida. He let Karen know he would be by the house in the afternoon. He went to leave Meg's house and walked out to the Subaru. Ensign got in, and he pulled out from the apartment parking lot. He only made it about fifty yards from the apartments and he pulled over alongside the curb.

Ensign had a flat tire on the back passenger side. His spare tire was situated beneath the bed he had made, a bunch of modifications, and all his luggage underneath everything in the hatchback. It took two hours in the cold to finally manage to free up the spare. A half hour after that, having changed the tire, squeezed the flat tire into the back of the car, and loaded his belongings into the back around it, Ensign was finally ready to drive. He checked his phone. He had a message from Karen an hour prior.

"You probably don't want to show up here now. The police are back."

Ensign called Karen. Officers had returned, and they found Tom hiding in a crawlspace. Karen's husband had set it up, but the officers needed visual confirmation that Tom was indeed the correct person wanted by North Carolina law enforcement. They arrested Tom on the spot, and they gave Karen a court summons to appear and answer for harboring a fugitive.

Had he not had a flat tire, Ensign would have arrived at Karen's house at the same time that incident happened. Ensign drove to a fast-food restaurant. He sat in his car and talked to Karen for an hour. Ensign decided he wasn't going to stop back at her house for his belongings. They were nothing important anyhow. Ensign tried his best to console Karen on the phone. He told her he would stay in touch as he was traveling. Ensign hung up the phone and headed to Ohio.

Ensign reached an auto supply store across the border in Ohio that evening. He bought a new high-performance car battery to support his camper-car's audio system. Ensign installed it while in the parking lot. He then drove another hour down to Adrian's house in Findlay. Ensign planned to stay there overnight, since the DMV was closed for the day. He decided he was going to drive back up to Perrysburg the next day to renew his driver's license, register his car, and get license plates.

Ensign handled all the car business the next day. He drove down to Adrian's house again. He had everything in order.

One more day, and he was going to leave for Florida. Ensign's dad lived in the Findlay area. Ensign hadn't seen him or talked to him in six years. For whatever reason early that next morning, as the Sun was rising, Ensign stopped at his dad's house.

What Goes Up...

"If I knew then what I know now…"

It was the beginning of 2021; everything going forth became extreme in ways Ensign could not have anticipated. Some of the highs yet to come were like nothing he had ever experienced. The lows…oh, the lows. Sometimes, rock bottom isn't just a point. Sometimes, you get dragged along the bottom, and you pray for it to end. You wish and hope for it to end, and you don't know if it will…

The drugs, stress, and adventure had already taken a toll on a brain unable to cope with what was a "normal" life…long before the adventure even began; a lifetime prior to 2018. Ensign's brain was broken from day one. The midlife crisis began when a tipping point culminated, when timing and events in life created that perfect storm.

That deal Ensign made with himself in 2018 was a last-ditched effort to not only create meaning, but to prolong a life self-condemned, a life doomed from the start. His life was meant to end one way or another in 2018. Upon that death, and only due to reaching that deal, something new was born.

Through all which had happened between that time he made that deal with himself back in 2018 up until the beginning of 2021, Ensign hadn't seen anything yet. His life had fallen apart many times over, but through it all; he finally felt alive. Ensign ascended an unimaginable arc. Through all the bad and unfortunate events, he somehow made it through. He reached a h point where he looked forward to what was next. Wonder excitement had him feeling alive through all the good and the bad.

Ensign didn't know anything at the dawn of 2021. It was a new year. He made it through external and internal turmoil, and he felt he had direction. Ensign didn't know that the direction was down. He didn't know the hardest two years of his life had just begun. Ensign didn't know...and he was nowhere near ready. That one ironic constant in life; it always changes. Life was, for sure, changing, and Ensign wasn't prepared. Even had he known what was coming, Ensign would have been steamrolled. He wasn't ready...and he almost didn't make it out alive.

9 798989 121854 *